CHARLES F. STANLEY BIBL

# DEEPENING YOUR PRAYER LIFE

## APPROACH GOD WITH BOLDNESS

# CHARLES F. STANLEY

THOMAS NELSON
*Since 1798*

DEEPENING YOUR PRAYER LIFE
CHARLES F. STANLEY BIBLE STUDY SERIES

Published in Nashville, Tennessee, by Thomas Nelson. Thomas Nelson is a registered trademark of HarperCollins Christian Publishing, Inc.

All Scripture quotations are taken from the New King James Version.® Copyright © 1982 by Thomas Nelson. Used by permission. All rights reserved worldwide.

Thomas Nelson titles may be purchased in bulk for educational, business, fundraising, or sales promotional use. For information, e-mail SpecialMarkets@ThomasNelson.com.

ISBN 978-0-310-10558-9 (softcover)
ISBN 978-0-310-10559-6 (ebook))

First Printing February 2020 / Printed in the United States of America

# CONTENTS

Introduction: Preparing to Communicate with God — 5

LESSON 1  Our Need to Communicate with God — 7

LESSON 2  God's Invitation to Prayer — 19

LESSON 3  Praying with Authority — 31

LESSON 4  The Warfare of Prayer — 43

LESSON 5  Prayer and Fasting — 55

LESSON 6  A Prayer Burden — 67

LESSON 7  Getting Answers to Prayer — 79

LESSON 8  Praying in the Will of God — 91

LESSON 9  Why Prayers Aren't Answered — 103

LESSON 10  Praying for Others — 115

LESSON 11  Time to Pray or Time to Act? — 127

LESSON 12  Prayer Is Where the Battle Is Won — 139

Leader's Guide — 151

# PREPARING TO COMMUNICATE WITH GOD

Prayer is communication. It is not a set of words or a memorized formula, nor is it an empty repetition of words and phrases. It is one person speaking with another—more specifically, one person speaking with God—and listening to what God has to say in return. This is true communication: two people speaking together, listening together, sharing themselves together.

Many good communication books are on the market today. The Bible, however, is God's foremost book about His communication with us. It is the source from which we receive new insights and eternal wisdom. It is the reference book to which we must continually return to make certain that what we hear from other people is acceptable to God and is true wisdom. You should read and study the Bible on a daily basis. It may be far more valuable for you to write what you learn from this study guide into the margins and end pages of your Bible than for you to write passages of the Bible or insights you have into this guide.

This book can be used by you alone or by several people in a small-group study. At various times, you will be asked to relate to the material in one of the following four ways.

*First, what new insights have you gained?* Make notes about the insights you have. You may want to record them in your Bible or in a separate journal. As you reflect on your new understanding, you are likely to see how God has moved in your life.

*Second, have you ever had a similar experience?* You approach the Bible from your own unique background . . . your own particular set of understandings about the world that you bring with you when you open God's Word. For this reason, it is important to consider how your experiences are shaping your understanding and allow yourself to be open to the truth that God reveals.

*Third, how do you feel about the material?* While you should not depend solely on your emotions as a gauge for your faith, it is important for you to be aware of them as you study a passage of Scripture and can freely express them to God. Sometimes, the Holy Spirit will use your emotions to compel you to look at your life in a different or challenging way.

*Fourth, in what way do you feel challenged to respond or to act?* God's Word may inspire you or challenge you to take a particular action. Take this challenge seriously and find ways to move into it. If God reveals a particular need that He wants *you* to address, take that as His "marching orders." God will empower you to *do* something with the challenge that He has just given you.

Start your Bible study sessions in prayer. Ask God to give you spiritual eyes to see and spiritual ears to hear. As you conclude your study, ask the Lord to seal what you have learned so you will not forget it. Ask Him to help you grow into the fullness of the nature and character of Christ Jesus.

I encourage you to keep the Bible at the center of your study. A genuine Bible study stays focused on God's Word and promotes a growing faith and a closer walk with the Holy Spirit in each person who participates.

# Our Need to Communicate with God

## IN THIS LESSON

*Learning:* What is prayer?

*Growing:* How should I pray?

*Prayer,* in its broadest definition, is communication with God. This includes both *verbal* and nonverbal *communication.* It covers your thoughts and actions toward God as well as the words you speak to your Creator. Prayer is a natural desire within you, for your Maker built this need to communication with Him into your being. It is part of His imprint on your life.

Based on this definition of prayer, some people may conclude that we are continually in communication with the Lord, because virtually everything we do is a message that we send to God or make before God. After all, God sees everything we do and knows everything we think and feel. From that vantage, our entire lives are prayers of a sort.

Others conclude we live continually in an atmosphere of prayer because God is always communicating with us. He sends messages about His great love for us. We have the Bible as His Word. He have messages that come through the loving actions and words of others. We have messages we perceive in the deep stirring of our spirits.

However, these two views of prayer are in error on one key point: *communication is a two-way* process. Simply sending a message is not communication. Communication requires that two parties respond to each other. Each party gives and receives messages and, in turn, provides feedback. A statement is made . . . and a specific response is provided. A question is asked . . . and an answer is given. Feelings are vented . . . and feelings are perceived in return.

True communication with God is not just talking *to* God but talking *with* God. You do not communicate if you merely voice a petition to God but do not wait for His answer. You do not communicate if you express your desires to God but do not hear what His desires are for you. You do not communicate if you vent your anger, frustration, or fears to God but do not listen for His response. Prayer is an active process involving two communicators: you and God.

**1.** What are your views on prayer? It is something that you feel you want to do, enjoy doing, or just a task to fulfill? Explain.

**2.** Are you satisfied or unsatisfied with the amount of time you spend in communication with God each week? Explain.

.................................................................................................

.................................................................................................

.................................................................................................

.................................................................................................

.................................................................................................

.................................................................................................

.................................................................................................

.................................................................................................

.................................................................................................

.................................................................................................

# PRAYER IS INTENTIONAL

At the outset of this study, there are few key points regarding prayer that we need to clarify. *First, prayer does not happen by accident.* You may express your prayers through feelings and thoughts, but prayer must be intentional for it truly to be a form of communication. You must actively engage in the process. You must turn your mind, heart, and voice toward God.

Voicing a concern to a friend is not prayer. Silently wishing that something might be so is not prayer. Confessing a fault to another person is not prayer. Feeling a spring in your step as you rejoice in the warmth and beauty of a summer day is not prayer. To be engaged in prayer, you must voice your thoughts to God with an expectation He will hear you and will respond.

To be engaged in prayer, you must yield your desires to God and expect Him to answer or change your desires as part of the process. To be in genuine prayer, you must make your confessions to God and actively receive His cleansing and forgiveness. To be a people of prayer, you must give voice to your thanksgiving and praise and open yourself fully to the presence of God at work in you and around you.

3. "Daniel . . . went home. And in his upper room, with his windows open toward Jerusalem, he knelt down on his knees three times that day, and prayed and gave thanks before his God, as was his custom since early days" (Daniel 6:10). What would you describe as your "custom" when it comes to your prayer habits?

_____

_____

_____

_____

_____

_____

4. What are some ways that you make prayer intentional in your life? What difficulties have you faced in doing this? What benefits have you received?

_____

_____

_____

_____

_____

_____

## PRAYER IS A DIALOGUE

*Second, prayer is a dialogue between you and God.* As you engage in prayer, you may voice to God your heartfelt cries of anguish, sorrow, pain, or give vent to your ecstatic joy. Likewise, God may give you a direction or speak a command to you. (Indeed, the Lord speaks when He wills to speak—and it is your responsibility to listen and obey.) At these times, you are talking to God or He is talking to you. This is *expression*, and it is valuable. However, it is not the most beneficial form of communication in a relationship.

Communication that builds relationships is *dialogue*. Genuine prayer has all the qualities and characteristics of a deeply meaningful conversation between two people. As God said to Isaiah, "Come now, and let us reason together" (Isaiah 1:18). This image of God and humans sitting down together for a good talk is our best image of prayer.

Can you imagine living in a relationship with a person who made demands but never waited to hear what you had to say? Such a relationship would be unfulfilling. You might establish a degree of civility and even work efficiently with that person, but the relationship would always be cold. This is precisely the nature of many people's prayer life. There is no heart to their communication with God, no real intimacy, and no deep fulfillment. For communication to be satisfying, it must involve a genuine dialogue . . . not a series of short monologues.

The end result of intentional dialogue can be wonderful. We know this to be true in our relationships with other people. When we have deep and heartfelt conversations with others, we often come away saying, "I have a much better understanding of them and their problems," "I have deeper feelings toward them," "I have a greater appreciation of them," or, "We have a stronger friendship." The same is true when you communicate intentionally and in dialogue with God. You know Him more fully, understand Him better, feel more at home in His presence, find cause to praise Him more, and have a deeper relationship with Him.

**5.** "Rest in the Lord, and wait patiently for Him" (Psalm 37:7). What are some ways that you *rest* in the Lord? How do you *wait* patiently for Him in prayer?

........................................................................

........................................................................

........................................................................

........................................................................

........................................................................

**6.** What are some of the things that God has revealed to you as you have engaged in a two-way dialogue with Him in prayer?

.............................................................................................................

.............................................................................................................

.............................................................................................................

.............................................................................................................

.............................................................................................................

.............................................................................................................

.............................................................................................................

.............................................................................................................

.............................................................................................................

.............................................................................................................

# PRAYER IS A DAILY PRIORITY

*Third, prayer is something we must make a daily priority in our lives.* Prayer is something we do on a continual basis. We are not to pray just when we run into crises or need immediate help. Rather, we are to pray daily—in both the good times and the bad.

In the Bible, we find Jesus often going off by Himself to spend time in prayer. In one story, we read that He spent an entire day in the city of Capernaum "[healing] many who were sick with various diseases, and [casting] out many demons" (Mark 1:34). But then, in the next verse, we read, "Now in the morning, having risen a long while before daylight, He went out and departed to a solitary place; and there He prayed" (verse 35).

I believe this was the habit of Jesus' life—to just get alone with God and just talk with Him about the events of the day. This was a habit that He made a priority . . . regardless of what situation He was facing. For instance, in another story, we read how Jesus—after learning of the death of John the Baptist—went away to a deserted place to spend time in prayer. But this time, the multitudes learned of His actions and "followed Him on foot from the cities" (Matthew 14:13).

Jesus had compassion for them and healed their sick. He also performed a miracle of feeding the 5,000-plus people with five loaves of bread and two fish.

Yet Jesus did not allow even this interruption to derail His time of prayer with the Father. After performing these miracles, we read that Jesus decided it was time to stop, send the multitudes away, get the disciples into a boat, and journey to the other side of the Sea of Galilee. "When He had sent the multitudes away, He went up on the mountain by Himself to pray" (verse 23). Jesus finished the day of service in prayer. Prayer was a priority.

The disciples watched Jesus perform these healings. They witnessed Him perform miracle after miracle and teach great spiritual truths to the people. But there was something unusual about Him whenever He came out of a place of prayer—and something about the *way* He prayed that they wanted to have in their own lives. Perhaps it was for this reason that one day they approached Jesus and asked, "Lord, teach us to pray" (Luke 11:1).

Jesus' response is what we know as the "Lord's Prayer." In this prayer, Jesus gives us a model for communicating with God on a daily basis. He begins by instructing us to praise God: "Our Father in heaven, hallowed be Your name." He asks for God's will to be done: "Your kingdom come. Your will be done on earth as it is in heaven." He instructs us to ask God to meet our needs: "Give us day by day our daily bread." He tells us to seek God's forgiveness and forgive others: "And forgive us our sins, for we also forgive everyone who is indebted to us." Jesus also states that we need to ask God for strength for the spiritual battles that we face: "And do not lead us into temptation, but deliver us from the evil one" (verses 2–4).

Jesus' life is a model of making prayer a daily priority. He prayed at His baptism. He prayed when He was tempted. He prayed before selecting His twelve disciples and on the night of His betrayal. He began His day in prayer, ended His day in prayer, and prayed for long stretches of time before making great decisions. All throughout

Jesus' life He was praying to His heavenly Father—and He was God. Shouldn't we follow His example and do the same?

**7.** How does Jesus' example of praying that we find throughout the Gospels match your own pattern of prayer? Explain.

 

**8.** Look again at Jesus' model prayer. What are some things for which you are thankful to God? What are some needs you need met? What are some ways you need His strength? Take a few minutes to write these down, and then take them to God in prayer.

 

# Prayer Is the Key to Relationship

Intentional dialogue with God will ultimately establish and deepen your relationship with Him. As Jesus demonstrated, the purpose of prayer is that you might know God better, experience more of His love, and have an abiding awareness of His work in your life. Talking *to* God doesn't build relationship. Communicating *with* God does.

A relationship with God, of course, is personal. In fact, it is the most intimate relationship you can ever know. Nobody knows you as God knows you. Nobody loves you as God loves you. Nobody desires good for your life more than God does. In prayer—in genuine communication with God—you soon discover more about God and more about yourself as God's beloved child. There is no greater exciting or enriching experience!

Your individual relationship with God is unique. This is true for every relationship that you have with another person, and it is no less true in your relationship with God. So, your prayers must be *your* prayers. Your communication with God is *your* communication. Written or formalized prayers have their place in certain group settings, but your times of communication with God should be marked by your own original speech. Prayer is talking with God as you would talk to your dearest friend, your most eager supporter, or your most loving mentor.

Given that prayer is intensely personal, there can be no universal formulas for it. For this reason, in this study we will not look at a series of procedures or offer a lockstep recipe for prayer. Rather, we will examine general principles that are basic to any person's prayer life. The specifics of your prayer relationship with God are as distinctive as any other aspect of your life and your ability to communicate.

As we approach this study in prayer, I encourage you to open yourself to the grand possibility that God has something to say to you that you will delight in hearing. He is eager to spend time with you and develop an intimate relationship with you that is marked by great joy. Ultimately, prayer is to be *experienced*, not studied. In study, we will simply learn how to better communicate with God—and to that end, how to have a better relationship with our Creator. It is an experience to be pursued and a relationship to be valued beyond all others.

**9.** "But know that the LORD has set apart for Himself him who is godly; the LORD will hear when I call to Him" (Psalm 4:3). What does it mean to call out to God? What promise are you given in this verse when you choose to do this in prayer?

**10.** "My sheep hear My voice, and I know them, and they follow Me" (John 10:27). In what areas of your life would you like to hear God's voice right now?

## TODAY AND TOMORROW

*Today:* Prayer is a dialogue between God and me—not just a monologue.

*Tomorrow:* I will spend time this week both talking and listening in prayer.

# CLOSING PRAYER

. . . . . . . . . . . . . . . . . . . . . . . . . . . . . . . . . . . . . . . . . . . . . .

*Heavenly Father, thank You for the pattern of the Lord Jesus Christ, who has taught us that early in the morning, late at night, and throughout the day we should be alone with You—being quiet and listening for Your voice. Help us to be intentional with our prayers and to make communicating with You— as a dialogue—a priority in our lives. We wait on You to do Your work in our hearts—pruning us, encouraging us, and enveloping us in Your love.*

# NOTES AND
# PRAYER REQUESTS

Use this space to write any key points, questions, or prayer requests from this week's study.

# God's Invitation to Prayer

*Learning:* What if God says no when I pray?

*Growing:* What should I do if I haven't received a clear answer to prayer?

Communication—or rather, failure to communicate—is a major problem in our world today. So often we don't say what we mean, have difficulty putting our feelings into words, and leave people with misunderstanding. We have problems communicating in the family, workplace, and the church. Many people also have problems communicating with God. They are uncomfortable speaking with Him, wonder if He has heard what they have said, or are confused or frustrated in their lack of ability to say what they mean.

However, the foremost problem is a failure to even *try* to communicate. Communication is stymied if we never open our mouths and hearts to others. Without an effort to start communicating, there can be no growth in our ability to communicate. This problem is not new. Repeatedly in the Bible, God invited His prophets to communicate with Him. He extends the same invitation to us. He asks us to start the process so that we can build a relationship.

In Jeremiah 33:1–3, we read, "Moreover the word of the LORD came to Jeremiah a second time, while he was still shut up in the court of the prison, saying, "Thus says the LORD who made it, the LORD who formed it to establish it (the LORD is His name): 'Call to Me, and I will answer you, and show you great and mighty things, which you do not know.'" Jeremiah was in prison for disagreeing with the leaders of Jerusalem who wanted to align themselves with the Egyptians to defeat the Babylonians, who were invading Israel.

The Lord had told Jeremiah that His people would be taken into captivity by the Babylonians for seventy years. Jeremiah therefore recommended that Israel surrender voluntarily. From his perspective, God's word was already coming to pass, so there was no point in fighting against it. But the leaders responded by putting Jeremiah in prison.

1. What did God command Jeremiah to do? What did He promise to do in response?

2. When has the Lord shown you "great and mighty things" as a result of prayer?

# "CALL TO ME"

There are three great messages in this word of the Lord to Jeremiah. First, God says, "Call to Me." There is probably no better place to catch up on one's prayer life than behind bars! We may not be behind physical bars, but we often are isolated through a series of events or problems and find ourselves feeling alone and captive to our circumstances. In those times, our attention often turns to God. Our cry is usually, "God, get me out of this situation!" Sometimes we may even attempt to barter with God, saying in effect, "God, get me out of here so I can serve You better and read the Scripture and pray more than I have in the past."

In reality, however, the "prison" in which we find ourselves may be the very place that God has designated for us to learn better how to serve Him, read the Bible, and pray more. This is especially true when the prison is one of our own making—a prison marked by our sin, emotional problems, relationship problems, self-created financial problems, or self-inflicted health problems. Our healing lies not in our deliverance from the problem but in developing a relationship with God in the midst of the problem.

God made no mention of Jeremiah's release from prison in this passage. He simply said, "Call to Me." God is far more interested in establishing a relationship with us and communicating with us within our situation than He is in changing our circumstances or releasing us from our problems. The lessons that we learn within life's problems are valuable for all eternity. They are greater than any lessons that we might learn from a miraculous deliverance from our pain or trouble.

God calls us to pray within the struggles of life. Prayer is the shortest distance between the problems and the solutions, difficulties and remedies, questions and answers. The distance between your knees and the floor is the shortest distance to seeing God actively at work in your life.

**3.** What is usually your first response when trouble strikes? How long does it usually take for you to turn to prayer?

......................................................................................................................

......................................................................................................................

......................................................................................................................

......................................................................................................................

**4.** What is usually your first response when blessings come to you? How often do you spend time in prayers of thanksgiving?

......................................................................................................................

......................................................................................................................

......................................................................................................................

......................................................................................................................

......................................................................................................................

# "I Will Answer You"

God wants us to come to Him as His beloved children so that He might be with us in every moment of our lives. He makes Himself personally available to us at any time of the day or night, no matter what we are facing. He says, "Call to Me. I am here." He promises, "I will answer you." We may not always sense His presence, but He is always there. People will often fail us in their promises to be there for us, but God will never fail us.

God has three main answers to our petitions: (1) *yes*, (2) *no*, and (3) *wait*. Each is an equally valid answer, though we don't always see them all that way. In truth, the only answer we often accept from God is *yes*. I frequently hear people say, "Praise God, He answered my prayer! He said yes to what I requested." I have never heard a person say with exuberance, "Praise God! He said no to what I requested!"

We want God to give us what we desire. But when God answers no, or wait, it is usually because we have not fully waited on Him to discover His will or direction for our lives. In such times, these answers will spare us heartache, keep us from error, or bring us growth so we will be ready to receive the fullness of God's blessing in our lives.

Of course, a *yes* answer is not guaranteed solely because we are living right. Sometimes, a *no* is necessary because God's answer to us affects another person who is not living right. What we can know with certainty is that God's answer is always for our protection and His motivation toward us is always love. He has our best interests at heart.

I know people who receive an answer from God they do not like and turn immediately to their Bibles in hope of finding another answer they like better. Some read aloud a verse of Scripture with the hope that God will change His mind. They are trying to get God to rethink His decision. This never works! God's answer is God's answer. We are wise to accept it.

If God says no, we are wise to ask Him if His reason for denying our request has to do with sin in our lives. We can ask Him to evaluate the desires of our hearts and show us which ones are not in keeping with His perfect plan. Likewise, if He tells us to wait, we are wise to be alert before God so that when the time is right, we can act to receive what God has for us.

In either case, we are submitting our lives to God, engaging in a process of communication, and opening ourselves up to a deeper relationship with Him. *No* and *wait* answers can be productive for our spiritual growth, even though they are seldom the answers that we want initially. Remember, God is more interested in our eternal future than in making us happy in the moment. God's answers are for our good, and He will not be swayed from giving us what is best for us. We simply do not have His perfect wisdom and understanding.

Our response to God's *no* and *wait* answers is critical. If we respond with submission, we are serving and relating to the Lord out of love. If we rebel, our relationship with Him and service to Him could be bound by duty, not love. God's desire, of course, is that His relationship with us be characterized by spontaneous love and devotion, not stubborn or prideful duty.

**5.** "My soul, wait silently for God alone, for my expectation is from Him" (Psalm 62:5). When has the Lord answered your prayer with *wait*? What insight does this verse offer in how to wait for God's answer?

**6.** "Because he has set his love upon Me, therefore I will deliver him; I will set him on high, because he has known My name. He shall call upon Me, and I will answer him; I will be with him in trouble; I will deliver him and honor him" (Psalm 91:14–15). What is required of us when we make requests to God?

## "SHOW YOU GREAT AND MIGHTY THINGS"

God invited Jeremiah to call to Him and then said, "I will answer you, and show you great and mighty things." Many of our petitions to God involve other people and our decisions related to them. We often ask God to bless our family members and friends and to exercise judgment on our enemies. But then we go about our daily business without ever considering what God might want *us* to do or what He might want to teach us and show us.

Note the things that God said He would show to Jeremiah. *First, He would show him great things.* God alone is truly great, and there is nothing greater than seeing God with spiritual eyes, hearing Him with spiritual ears, and gaining an understanding of what He is able to do. God alone knows our past deeds and our future potential. He is the Holy One, the great Creator, Sustainer, and Lover of mankind. God wanted to show Himself to Jeremiah. He wanted to reveal what was possible for Jeremiah's future and the future of all God's people.

When we read the Bible , we see the greatness of God on virtually every page. When we look at the lives of great Christians through the ages, we see the greatness of God at work. When we reflect back over the experiences of our own lives, we have evidence of God's greatness. God wants to show us His own greatness. He wants to communicate to us His vast love and power and wisdom—all of which He makes available to us.

*Second, God said that He would show Jeremiah mighty things.* He promised to reveal "mighty things, which you do not know." The word *mighty* in our current English usage does not mean what it meant at this time. The term usually referred to great fortified cities—ones that were walled in. It was a reference to things that are hidden, secret, and secure.

God desires to reveal to us the things that are inaccessible through any means except prayer. It is through our communication with God that He reveals the secret treasures of understanding and discernment that are "hidden" in the Scriptures. It is through our conversations with God that He reveals the unknown answers to our questions and the solutions to our problems. When we come to the Lord with a pure and humble heart, He can trust us with the precious riches of His power.

I have gone to God repeatedly through the years to ask for guidance and direction. Many times, His answer involved things that had been hidden to me. God led me to ask questions that I would not otherwise have asked, to seek information that I would not otherwise have sought, to probe issues that I would not otherwise have touched, and to contact people that I would not otherwise have called. In the process of obeying God's guidance, He has given me access to resources and ideas and solutions that were previously unknown to me. In every instance, what God revealed was for my ultimate and eternal good. I have no doubt that what God has done for me, He will do for you.

God's revelation of mighty things may not come quickly. In some cases, we may not yet be able to receive the information or make full use of the resources revealed to us. But God will not keep from us anything that we need to know. He responds to our cries for help by revealing Himself as the source of all our help and also by supplying all the resources we need.

**7.** What is the difference between the "great things" and the "mighty things" that God reveals through prayer?

**8.** Spend time right now in prayer, asking the Lord to reveal to you the great things and mighty things that He wants to show you. What do you sense Him saying to you?

# THE INVITATION TO KNOCK, ASK, SEEK

Jesus reissued God's invitation to "call to Me" when He said, "Ask, and it will be given to you; seek, and you will find; knock, and it will be opened to you" (Matthew 7:7). Jesus' promise to His followers is just as sure as the one God made to Jeremiah: the one who asks, seeks, and knocks will receive His answer and supply.

Asking, seeking, and knocking are all aspects of our prayer life. *First, we are to ask for the things we need.* Some people seem reluctant to pray for the material goods and resources they need, but God invites us to do so. In fact, He tells us that we often don't have what we need because we haven't asked (see James 4:2).

*Second, we are to seek understanding and knowledge so that we can develop relationships with others.* The goal of seeking is to find someone, and our primary goal is to seek God. *Third, we are to knock on the doors of opportunity that appear before us.* We are to respond in faith to the potential for good that God places in our paths. God wants us to fulfill the potential that He has placed in us. He wants us to feel satisfaction and fulfillment in what we do for Him and through Him.

The basis for all answered prayer is God's love. He responds to our petitions for things, relationships, and fulfillment because He loves us. Our asking, seeking, and knocking are all to be done within the context of our ongoing daily communication with God. Our needs change daily. New opportunities come our way on a daily basis. Relationships are built day by day. Therefore, our communication with God must be daily.

Jesus referred to this daily intimate relationship as *abiding* in God. The communication of a person who is abiding is frequent, without barriers, and deeply personal and meaningful. As we develop that kind of communication with God, He will reveal to us and provide for us all that we can possibly desire, in part because our desires will be His desires for us.

**9.** "For everyone who asks receives, and he who seeks finds, and to him who knocks it will be opened" (Matthew 7:8). What are some examples of *asking*, *seeking*, and *knocking* as they apply to prayer?

**10.** What are your responsibilities in prayer? What would you say are God's responsibilities when it comes to prayer?

## TODAY AND TOMORROW

*Today:* God sometimes asks us to wait for His answer, and He wants us to trust Him in that time.

*Tomorrow:* I will ask the Lord to show me great and mighty things through prayer.

# CLOSING PRAYER

*Father, we thank You for loving us enough to provide for us. We thank You for not only providing physical things and material things, but also for providing Your wisdom and Your knowledge. We need to know Your will in the decisions that we make and know Your sense of direction. Grant us the faith to be obedient to whatever You require of us, whatever the solution may be. And teach us how to talk with You. This we ask in Jesus' name.*

# Notes and
# Prayer Requests

Use this space to write any key points, questions, or prayer requests from this week's study.

# PRAYING WITH AUTHORITY

## IN THIS LESSON

*Learning:* Who gives us authority to pray in the first place?

*Growing:* Where does the power of prayer come from?

The prophet Elijah and King Ahab had been in conflict over idolatry and false worship in Israel. Then Elijah declared a showdown. He commanded the king to call the Israelites to Mount Carmel and summon the prophets of Baal and Asherah, who were supported by Queen Jezebel. When all parties were assembled, Elijah said to the people, "How long will you falter between two opinions? If the LORD is God, follow Him; but if Baal, follow him" (1 Kings 18:21).

The people did not respond, so Elijah challenged the prophets of Baal and Asherah to a sort of duel. The prophets and Elijah were each given a bull to sacrifice. Elijah said, "You call on the name of your gods, and I will call on the name of the LORD; and the God who answers by fire, He is God" (verse 24). The prophets agreed to this plan. They spent all day crying out to Baal, leaping about and cutting themselves with knives, but to avail.

Meanwhile, Elijah took twelve stones and made an altar. He surrounded the altar with a trench and then soaked the firewood and the sacrificial bull with water until the trench was also filled with water. In fact, he soaked the wood and sacrifice with water three times! At the time of the evening sacrifice, Elijah prayed, "Lord God of Abraham, Isaac, and Israel, let it be known this day that You are God in Israel and I am Your servant, and that I have done all these things at Your word. Hear me, O Lord, hear me, that this people may know that You are the Lord God, and that You have turned their hearts back to You again" (verses 36–37).

When Elijah had finished, the fire of the Lord fell and consumed the sacrifice, wood, stones, the dust, and all the water in the trench. When the people saw what had happened, they fell on their faces and said, "The Lord, He is God! The Lord, He is God!" (verse 39). What a wonderful example of praying with boldness and authority! Elijah didn't pray in secret, off in some corner where nobody could see him. He prayed openly and publicly. There was nothing tricky or shady about what he did. There was no doubt about what he said.

A man once said to me, "I feel that when I come into the throne room of God, I just tiptoe around. I'm afraid of what God may say or do." I believe his behavior is that of many Christians. However, God tells us to come boldly into His presence. He grants us the privilege to come before Him with authority because of our position in Christ Jesus. We are to be bold in believing that God is going to do what He says He will do in our lives.

1. "We do not have a High Priest who cannot sympathize with our weaknesses, but was in all points tempted as we are, yet without sin. Let us therefore come boldly to the throne of grace, that we may obtain mercy and find grace to help in time of need" (Hebrews 4:15–16). What is the connection between the fact that

Jesus was tempted and the boldness with which you can enter God's presence?

_____

_____

_____

_____

_____

_____

**2.** Why is it comforting to know that Jesus was tempted in the same ways that you are? How does this help Him to "sympathize with our weaknesses"?

_____

_____

_____

_____

_____

_____

# OUR POSITION BEFORE GOD

In another story told in the Bible, we read about an assault launched against King Jehoshaphat and the people of Israel. Jehoshaphat was afraid, but rather than cower in fear, he "set himself to seek the Lord" (2 Chronicles 20:3). He proclaimed a fast and called the people to join him in seeking the Lord. He stood before them and prayed, "O LORD God of our fathers, are You not God in heaven, and do You not rule over all the kingdoms of the nations, and in Your hand is there not power and might, so that no one is able to withstand You?" (verse 6).

Jehoshaphat was not doubting the power of God . . . rather, he was affirming his belief in the Lord. He was declaring that he was putting all of his trust in the God of unlimited power. He went on to state in his prayer that he was standing in a position of humility and weakness before the Lord. He told God that He was the one who had given the land to the Israelites and had allowed them to dwell there and build a sanctuary in it. He said that God had told them to cry out to Him in their affliction—and that He would save them.

Jehoshaphat also told God that He was the one who had instructed them to spare these enemy people when they first came to occupy this land and that He was the only one capable of judging these enemies—they had no power and no plan (see verses 7–12). He concluded by stating the eyes of the Israelites were squarely on the Lord and on no other god.

Jehoshaphat was saying, "Lord, if You do not exercise Your authority in this matter, we are all doomed. So we are putting our entire trust and confidence in You and You alone." There was no trace of egotism in Jehoshaphat. He claimed no authority in himself and also no power for himself.

**3.** Why did Jehoshaphat remind the Lord of the things that He had done for Israel in the past? How can you do the same by quoting Scripture in prayer?

**4.** What did Jehoshaphat mean when he said, "Our eyes are upon You"? How can you imitate this attitude in prayer?

# OUR AUTHORITY AND POWER IN PRAYER

Jesus gave the following instructions to His disciples in what is known as the Great Commission:

> All authority has been given to Me in heaven and on earth. Go therefore and make disciples of all the nations, baptizing them in the name of the Father and of the Son and of the Holy Spirit, teaching them to observe all things that I have commanded you; and lo, I am with you always, even to the end of the age (Matthew 28:18–20).

The word *power* in this passage refers to the ability to bring about, execute, or act with hindrances removed. It refers to a divine capacity—a divine right or privilege. Jesus was declaring He had the authority to send out His own disciples.

In Acts 1:8, the word *power* is translated from the Greek word *dunamis*: "But you shall receive power [*dunamis*] when the Holy Spirit has come upon you; and you shall be witnesses to Me in Jerusalem, and in all Judea and Samaria, and to the end of the earth." This word refers to the *dynamic ability* that will be given to the disciples so that they can be witnesses. This is an enabling and highly effective power.

Jesus was not turning over the fullness of His authority to His disciples—He retains His authority as Savior and Lord always. What He was imparting to His disciples (through the Holy Spirit) was the ability to do whatever He authorized them to do. His disciples would receive the power through the Holy Spirit to carry out the mission that Jesus was sending them on. Jesus is the one who possesses the authority and imparts the ability through the Holy Spirit.

This is a critical distinction for us to make. As Christians, we do not have authority in ourselves. All authority resides in Jesus, our Savior and Lord. But we have been given power to carry out Jesus' commandments on earth. Furthermore, we do not have this power in ourselves apart from the Holy Spirit. It is a power that is given to us by Jesus, and which we must actively receive from the Spirit.

Both words, *authority* and *power*, are recorded in Luke 9:1: "Then He called His twelve disciples together and gave them power and authority over all demons, and to cure diseases." Jesus sent out His twelve disciples to preach the kingdom of God and gave them power and authority for a ministry of healing and deliverance. He imparted to them the capacity for this type of ministry and the power to do this ministry. In other words, He gifted them with both the *can-do* authority and *will-succeed* power.

Jesus expected His disciples to fulfill their mission because they had been equipped to do so. The same is true for us. When God sends us on a mission, He gives us the ability to do it and the power to accomplish it. He gives us the authority to pray and empowers us to pray. He moves in us and through us by the Holy Spirit so that our prayers are effective. The believer who prays in Atlanta can be effective in bringing about spiritual change in Tehran. The believer who prays in southern California can be effective in bringing about God's blessing on the church in China. There is no distance in prayer. Prayer can affect any situation, alter any circumstance, and bring about any type of change anywhere on earth.

Prayer is both a commandment of God and a mission. God has given us the privilege to call on His name at any place and any time. He has given us the name of Jesus—the greatest name on earth and in heaven—as our authority in which to pray. Nothing allows us any greater potential to affect the state of an individual sinful heart and the state of world affairs. Prayer is the most potent, effective, life-changing force given by God to humankind. It is up to us, therefore, to pray—and to pray boldly and with the full force of our faith in Christ Jesus.

**5.** "Whatever we ask we receive from Him, because we keep His commandments and do those things that are pleasing in His sight" (1

John 3:22). What are you required to do if you wish to receive what you ask for from God? Give practical examples.

.................................................................................................

.................................................................................................

.................................................................................................

.................................................................................................

.................................................................................................

.................................................................................................

.................................................................................................

**6.** What is the implication of this verse if you *don't* do those things?

.................................................................................................

.................................................................................................

.................................................................................................

.................................................................................................

.................................................................................................

.................................................................................................

# OUR OFFENSE AGAINST THE ENEMY

When you begin to pray with power, the enemy of your soul will come to you and say, "Why do you think you have the right to pray for that? Who do you think you are?" Paul addressed this matter in his letter to the Ephesians. He said they must adopt a posture of boldness in prayer: "Be strong in the Lord and in the power of His might" (6:10). Paul stated their authority and power were imparted by Christ Jesus. They were not bold or powerful in their own right.

He then reminded the Ephesians their ever-present enemy was Satan. You are in mortal conflict with the devil and his demons. You battle against the wiles of the devil and wrestle against principalities, powers, rulers of the darkness of this age, and spiritual hosts of wickedness (see verses 11–12). Whenever you begin to pray, you can expect

Satan to put up a fight against your prayers. So, how are you overcome to him?

Paul said that you are to "take up the whole armor of God, that you may be able to withstand in the evil day, and having done all, to stand" (verse 13). He described this armor as (1) the breastplate of righteousness, (2) shoes of the preparation of the gospel of peace, (3) the shield of faith (by which you are able to quench all the fiery darts of the enemy), (4) the helmet of salvation, and (5) the sword of the Spirit, which is the word of God (see verses 14–17).

When you put on the whole armor of God, you are putting on the identity of Christ. You are recognizing that Jesus alone is your authority. He is your righteousness and your peace. The Author and Finisher of your faith. He is your Savior and the one who reminds you of the word of God and teaches you the deep meanings of God's Word. He has the full capacity to defeat the enemy at every turn, and He has imparted to you the capacity to defeat the enemy at specific times and places through your prayers.

Paul closed this illustration by stating you are to pray always "with all prayer and supplication in the Spirit, being watchful to this end with all perseverance and supplication for all the saints" (verse 18). Prayer is your offense against the devil's attacks and against his strongholds. You have the power of the Holy Spirit working in you to make certain you are able to exercise the authority of Christ successfully. Paul declared this to be a winning posture. You will not fail against the devil if you recognize the real enemy, put on the armor of Christ, and take on the authority that He alone imparts to you, and then pray with persevering faith.

None of us has the authority or the power to stand against the devil on the basis of our own personality, intellect, or gifts. But in Christ, we have His authority and His power to soundly defeat the enemy regardless of what he may launch against us. What a contrast this is to simply wishing and hoping in prayer that God will act! We must understand that God wants bold and assertive action in prayer. He wants us to pray as if we are fighting and defeating the most real of all enemies—not only in our personal lives but also on behalf of other believers.

**7.** Consider each of these pieces of armor that Paul lists in Ephesians 6:14–18. What is the purpose of the breastplate, shoes, shield, helmet, and sword?

..............................................................................................................................

..............................................................................................................................

..............................................................................................................................

..............................................................................................................................

..............................................................................................................................

..............................................................................................................................

**8.** What element of your Christian faith is pictured by each of these pieces of armor?

..............................................................................................................................

..............................................................................................................................

..............................................................................................................................

..............................................................................................................................

..............................................................................................................................

..............................................................................................................................

..............................................................................................................................

# Praying with Perseverance

Paul concluded by admonishing the Ephesians to pray "always . . . being watchful to this end with all perseverance" (6:18). Jesus repeatedly told His disciples to "watch and pray." Knowing that we have the authority in Christ and the power to pray successfully means very little if we do not pray. Our command from God is to pray and to do so boldly and consistently, relying totally on Him and exercising the full authority and power given to us by Jesus.

**9.** "Praying always with all prayer and supplication in the Spirit, being watchful to this end with all perseverance and supplication for all the saints" (Ephesians 6:18). Why is perseverance important in prayer?

**10.** Who are "all the saints"? How can you be praying for all the saints this week?

## TODAY AND TOMORROW

*Today:* The Lord has given me the authority to pray through the work of Christ Jesus.

*Tomorrow:* I will spend time each day this week putting on my armor of Christ.

# CLOSING PRAYER

. . . . . . . . . . . . . . . . . . . . . . . . . . . . . . . . . . . . . . . . . . . . . . . .

*Father, we thank You for loving us and for being patient with us. Continue to teach us today the knowledge of Your Word and instruct us on the incredible authority that we have been given in prayer. Speak to our hearts and help us to see the tremendous potential that is within us if we simply choose to use what is at our fingertips—to apply what You, in Your mercy, have given to us. We thank You for loving us and pray that You will speak to our hearts today.*

# NOTES AND PRAYER REQUESTS

· · · · · · · · · · · · · · · · · · · · · · · · · · · · · · · · · · · · · · · · ·

Use this space to write any key points, questions, or prayer requests from this week's study.

# The Warfare of Prayer

## IN THIS LESSON

*Learning:* What is a satanic stronghold?

*Growing:* What steps can I take to identify and remove any satanic strongholds in my life?

Imagine the year is 1944. You are a soldier in the U.S. army, and you are on an amphibious vessel about to land at Omaha Beach in Normandy. (Historians will later refer to the battle as D-Day.) Picture yourself on that boat with your fellow soldiers. You turn to the man near you and say, "I hear this battle could turn the tide of the whole war."

To your surprise, the soldier looks back at you and asks, "What war?" You decide to humor the fellow, so you say, "The war we're fighting against the Nazis." The man has a puzzled expression on his face. "What is a Nazi?" he asks you.

I would guess this poor soldier would be in for a rather nasty surprise. If you are in a war, but you don't realize you are in a war, it is quite likely that you are going to get wounded. If you are in a war and don't know who your enemy is, you are working at a terrible disadvantage. And if the enemy has a base right in your front door, and you are not even aware that it is there, you are bound to be defeated!

Unfortunately, this is the situation many of us in the church are dealing with today. We are in a war against a serious enemy—a deadly enemy—yet many of us don't realize it. And even if we do understand it intellectually, we don't *live* as if we are in the midst of a war. Again, as the apostle Paul explained, "We do not wrestle against flesh and blood, but against principalities, against powers, against the rulers of the darkness of this age, against spiritual hosts of wickedness in the heavenly places" (Ephesians 6:12).

There is one aspect of spiritual warfare in the body of Christ that is especially misunderstood today—or even ignored. This is what Paul referred to as "strongholds." Here is what he said in another letter: "For the weapons of our warfare are not carnal but mighty in God for pulling down strongholds" (2 Corinthians 10:4). The Greek word Paul uses for *stronghold* in this verse describes a fortified castle. Paul is not talking about *physical* castles but *rather* spiritual fortifications that exist in our lives. A stronghold is a spiritual power base occupied by our enemy that has the potential to be incredibly destructive.

In this session, we will to explore the reality of these strongholds, including how they impact our prayer lives and how we can use prayer as a weapon to tear them down. As we do, we will address: (1) what Satan's designs are for these strongholds, (2) how strongholds develop in our lives, and (3) how we can in turn demolish these strongholds.

**1.** How would you summarize what you have been taught about spiritual warfare?

**2.** Why do you think many believers in the church today are unaware that a spiritual battle—such as the one Paul describes in Ephesians 6:10–20—is taking place?

.................................................................................

.................................................................................

.................................................................................

.................................................................................

# SATAN'S DESIGN FOR STRONGHOLDS

Satan and his forces are the source of these spiritual strongholds. But what is Satan's ultimate objective for building and maintaining a stronghold in your life? On the surface, his motivation is simple: he wants to cause you harm and distract you from God's purposes and plans. But there are also some specific strategies that Satan has in mind when he spots a weakness in your life and attempts to build a stronghold on that point.

*First, Satan's design is to divide your mind.* If Satan harasses you in a particular area or discovers some area of weakness in which he can work, it will divide your thoughts. Let's say, for example, that you have a stronghold of jealousy. Maybe there is somebody in your life for whom Satan has warped your attitude. You think that person is better than you are and that he or she is trying to get the best of you. Satan can use that stronghold to divide your mind. You will be thinking about something else and all of a sudden that person will pop in your thoughts. It can happen continually. Satan will harass you by regularly whispering, "That person is better. That person is more successful. That person is conspiring behind your back."

*Second, Satan's design is to discourage you.* The enemy will constantly remind you of your failures and your mistakes—especially your sins. "Look," he will say to you, "you've gone and done it again. How could God love someone who does that? Don't you know that God is ashamed of you? Don't you know God is disappointed with you?"

If you don't understand what is happening, you will start agreeing with the enemy's lies. You will start to believe what Satan says about you over what God says about you. It will cause discouragement.

*Finally, Satan's design is to disillusion you.* Once you are feeling distracted and discouraged, he will keep attacking you in that same place again and again. After all, why would he stop when it works so well? His goal is to get you to think, "I don't believe this Christian life works. I've confessed my sins, I've repented, I've read the Bible, I've been to revival meetings, I've been to seminars, I've been to Bible conferences, I've been to Bible studies, I've been to prayer groups—but I'm still dealing with the same old problems, and nothing seems to work."

It is easy to get disillusioned by the enemy's constant attacks and disillusioned by your own sense of failure. Just think of how many times you have prayed, "God, I promise on a stack of Bibles that I will not do this anymore!" How long did that promise last? Thirty minutes? A few days? The reason it did not work is because it is not how you deal with a stronghold. You are attacking the problem the wrong way. And your continued failure makes you feel disillusioned.

**3.** What are the biggest sources of discouragement in your life?

.......................................................................................................

.......................................................................................................

.......................................................................................................

.......................................................................................................

.......................................................................................................

**4.** Are there any areas of life right now where you feel distracted, discouraged, or disillusioned?

.......................................................................................................

.......................................................................................................

.......................................................................................................

.......................................................................................................

.......................................................................................................

# How Strongholds Develop

The first thing to know about strongholds is that they can happen both *involuntarily* and *voluntarily*. An involuntary stronghold can develop and take hold as a result of something that is programmed into your thinking by others. It's not your choice. This typically happens during your younger years. The people you believe or respect feed false ideas or false beliefs into your mind . . . and eventually they take root and develop into a power base for the enemy.

For example, let's say you grew up in a home where your parents didn't get along, your brothers and sisters fought all the time, and as a result you were the object of continuous criticism. You endured that criticism until you became an adult—but it affected you. It impacted you. You often felt you were no good, that you would never succeed at life, and that you would never get the kinds of breaks other people enjoyed. This represents an area of weakness, and Satan will take advantage of it. Satan will still use those lies that other people spoke into your life as footholds of self-doubt to build a stronghold of accusation in your mind.

Voluntary strongholds are different, because they are the result of your own choices—the result of your sins. Every stronghold begins with a *thought*. It may be a thought about greed, jealousy, lust, or anything else . . . but it always begins with a thought. "I want that. I deserve that. I should have that." The thought then moves to *consideration*. Once the thought enters your mind, you begin to dwell on it. You begin to look at all the aspects of it, just like you might turn a jewel round and round in your fingers to see all the different facets. You allow that thought to turn in your mind, as if you are chewing on it and savoring it.

Next, this consideration becomes an *attitude*. The more you think about something, the more you are prone to start thinking in that direction. Soon it becomes an attitude—a part of your mindset and your thought patterns—and then it turns into an *action*. After all, if you think about something long enough and you lean in that direction long enough—you are eventually going to do something about it. The attitude is going to become an action.

When this action is repeated again and again, it transforms into a *habit*. It becomes something you turn to regularly. Something you almost feel as if you can't live without. Finally, the habit becomes a *stronghold*. It becomes a fortification of Satan in your own mind and heart—a place from which he can attack you with impunity.

**5.** As you look back on your life, are there any messages or labels that have "stuck" after being spoken into your life by others? How do these represent strongholds?

_____

_____

_____

_____

_____

_____

**6.** How do you react to this six-step process of how voluntary strongholds develop? Do the steps ring true for you? Explain.

_____

_____

_____

_____

_____

_____

# IDENTIFYING STRONGHOLDS

At this point in the study, you might be asking, "Do I have one of these strongholds in my life?" There are several ways you can determine if any strongholds exist.

First, think of any area or place in your life about which you make these statements: "I don't know why I keep doing that. I don't know why I keep thinking that. I don't know why I can't gain any ground in this area." If so, you have identified a stronghold. Second, look for anything you consistently do in excess or take to excess. This could be eating, seeking pleasure, gossiping, judging others, or stockpiling money (which is greed). Anything that you do in excess is a like a neon sign flashing, "stronghold!"

Prayer can help you to identify strongholds. It's best if you regularly take moments throughout the day to quiet yourself before God and seek His guidance. Just simply ask Him, "Lord, where do you see strongholds in my life? What are the areas where I keep doing things and I don't understand why? Where am I taking things to excess?"

Prayer is a critical tool for identifying strongholds. And, as we will see next, prayer is a critical tool for *demolishing* strongholds.

**7.** What is an area (or areas) of life where you say, "I don't understand why I do that"?

......................................................................................................

......................................................................................................

......................................................................................................

......................................................................................................

......................................................................................................

......................................................................................................

**8.** Where do you see yourself regularly struggling with taking things to excess?

......................................................................................................

......................................................................................................

......................................................................................................

......................................................................................................

......................................................................................................

......................................................................................................

# DEMOLISHING STRONGHOLDS

So, how do you eliminate strongholds in your life? This is the key question that you need to be asking. I believe the answer can be found in Paul's words recorded in 2 Corinthians 10:4–5:

> For the weapons of our warfare are not carnal but mighty in God for pulling down strongholds, casting down arguments and every high thing that exalts itself against the knowledge of God, bringing every thought into captivity to the obedience of Christ.

The weapons you use to attack and destroy the strongholds in your life are *divine* weapons. They are supernatural weapons. And it all starts with prayer. Talk about deepening your prayer life! There are not many experiences with prayer that can compare with attacking the enemy head-on and destroying his fortified power bases.

*To begin, familiarize yourself with the Scriptures.* Specifically, seek out those passages that address strongholds you want to pull down. For example, if your stronghold is lust, memorize passages such as 1 Corinthians 6:18: "Flee sexual immorality. Every sin that a man does is outside the body, but he who commits sexual immorality sins against his own body." If your stronghold involves jealousy or hatred or bitterness, find Scripture passages that address those themes. When you do, God will bring those Scriptures to mind as you pray. They will be powerful weapons both to defend against temptation and as you go on the attack.

*Second, pray in the name of Jesus.* Satan cannot tolerate our Savior's name. It is the "name which is above every name" (Philippians 2:9). When Peter and John were confronted by the beggar at the gate of the temple, Peter told him, "Silver and gold I do not have, but what I do have I give you: In the name of Jesus Christ of Nazareth, rise up and walk" (Acts 3:6). If you want to destroy the strongholds in your life, you need to approach the demolition process through the authority of Jesus Christ and in the power of His name.

*Third, rely on the blood of Christ that was shed on the cross.* Satan will not give up his strongholds easily. He will fight and do whatever he can to hold on to them. But the Bible states that Satan will be overcome "by the blood of the Lamb and by the word of their testimony" (Revelation 12:11).

In the book of Exodus, the angel of death came like a fog moving over the nation of Egypt. The firstborn was killed wherever the lamb's blood did not appear on the door. The blood of Jesus has always been a source of protection for God's people. Not only that, but Jesus' blood is also your means of access to the throne of God. You not only pray in the *name* of Jesus but also under the *protection* and *power* of His blood that was shed on the cross.

*The final weapon in demolishing strongholds is the Holy Spirit.* According to 1 John 4:4, "He who is in you is greater than he who is in the world." Who is the "He" inside you? The Holy Spirit. He carries the power you need. He is your advocate and will give you the firepower to not only identify the strongholds in our lives but also tear them down.

As you tear down these strongholds, it is important for you to be honest about what you are doing. Call the stronghold by name. Acknowledge you are in the middle of spiritual warfare. Be honest about what your stronghold is and how it developed in your life. Approach this process under the umbrella of faith. It is not God's will for Satan to maintain strongholds in your life—and you need to *believe* it is not. It is the will of God for you to have victory over the darkness in your spiritual life. It is the will of God for any and all strongholds in your mind and heart to be torn down, smashed, and demolished once and for all.

Believe that truth in faith. Attack those strongholds with the supernatural weapons you have been given. And you will see these strongholds begin to fall.

**9.** How would you describe your experiences with using these weapons in the past?

**10.** On a practical level, what does it look like to access the protection of Jesus' blood and the power of the Holy Spirit?

## TODAY AND TOMORROW

*Today:* I have access to the weapons I need for tearing down any and all strongholds in my life.

*Tomorrow:* I will make it a priority to work in God's power to prevent new strongholds from developing in the months and years to come.

# CLOSING PRAYER

. . . . . . . . . . . . . . . . . . . . . . . . . . . . . . . . . . . . . . . . . . . . . . . . . . .

*Father, we thank You and praise You that you have not left us susceptible to Satan's tricks—his snares, his manipulations, his conniving—but you have warned us against them. You have said that we are fighting against principalities and powers . . . against satanic power. But You have also promised there is a greater power within us than the one who is in the world! We know Your Holy Spirit within us is more powerful than all the satanic forces in all the earth, in all the universe, in all the worlds that there may be. Help us to exert that power and authority today.*

# NOTES AND
# PRAYER REQUESTS

Use this space to write any key points, questions, or prayer requests from this week's study.

# PRAYER AND FASTING

## IN THIS LESSON

*Learning:* What is the point of prayer and fasting?

*Growing:* How do I know if God is calling me to spend time in fasting?

Our motivation as believers in Christ is always to express love—love for God and for others. Our behavior must never be rooted in pride or displayed so we draw attention to ourselves. Jesus made this clear in the Sermon on the Mount in regard to three particular areas of Christian behavior: almsgiving, prayer, and fasting (see Matthew 6:5–8, 16–18).

In a previous lesson, we discussed two examples of prayer—Elijah's prayer before the prophets of Baal and Jehoshaphat's prayer before the people of Israel. In those two examples, the leaders openly expressed their faith and trust in God alone. These men represent bold examples of giving public witness through prayer—and a bold witness through prayer can only be made if it is the outgrowth of countless hours of private and personal prayer.

God desires to know us best. He is a jealous God who insists on being the foremost object of our affection and loyalty. When we pray, we are invited to disclose our innermost thoughts, feelings, and desires to Him alone. Sharing our secrets and desires in this manner results in a relationship with God. As we share, we open ourselves up to His healing, guiding, and comforting power and presence. In contrast, public displays of prayer performed primarily to draw attention to oneself do nothing to further a relationship with the Lord God.

Jesus said, "When you pray, you shall not be like the hypocrites. For they love to pray standing in the synagogues and on the corners of the streets, that they may be seen by men. Assuredly, I say to you, they have their reward" (Matthew 6:5). Jesus said the same for public displays of fasting: "Moreover, when you fast, do not be like the hypocrites, with a sad countenance. For they disfigure their faces that they may appear to men to be fasting. Assuredly, I say to you, they have their reward" (verse 16).

Such open displays bring attention solely to the person and not to God. The purpose of prayer and fasting is not that others might applaud us but that we might be changed and transformed. The Bible has repeated references to this "secret" nature of our relationship with God. This does not mean we are to deny our relationship with God or keep our witness for Christ under wraps. Rather, our relationship with God is to be intimate. It is intensely personal and private. When we have a deep relationship with the Lord, we can then speak and act publicly as He directs.

1. "When you pray, go into your room, and when you have shut your door, pray to your Father who is in the secret place; and your Father who sees in secret will reward you openly" (Matthew 6:6).

Why would some people want to be seen praying in public? What would be their motivation? Their "reward"?

.................................................................................

.................................................................................

.................................................................................

.................................................................................

.................................................................................

.................................................................................

**2.** "When you pray, do not use vain repetitions as the heathen do. For they think that they will be heard for their many words" (Matthew 6:7). What are "vain repetitions" in prayer? Why are Christians to avoid such types of prayer?

.................................................................................

.................................................................................

.................................................................................

.................................................................................

.................................................................................

.................................................................................

.................................................................................

# THE PURPOSE OF PRAYER AND FASTING

The Word of God, our faith, praise, the name of Jesus, and the blood of Jesus are all weapons in our spiritual warfare against evil. Yet prayer and fasting are two of our *foremost* weapons in our battle against Satan. For this reason, we must be sure to use these weapons correctly.

*First, we must not use prayer and fasting to avoid doing God's will.* Some people turn to prayer and fasting as a substitute for obedient action. They think they can convince themselves (and God) that they are being obedient by praying and fasting about a situation, when in reality they are avoiding the business that God has called them to do.

*Second, we must not think prayer and fasting are a substitute for repenting of sin.* Some people think they can continue to sin if they balance it with a proper amount of prayer and fasting. Only the shed blood of Jesus Christ can provide atonement for sin. Prayer and fasting might strengthen our ability to turn away from sin and not give in to temptation, but they are not an antidote or a compensation for sin.

The real purpose for fasting is to bring the body and soul into subjection so that in prayer we can be focused solely on God and His plans and purposes for our lives. Each of us has natural desires and appetites that are a part of our creation. These are to be satisfied in proper ways according to God's commandments so the fulfillment of our desires and appetites brings about good to our bodies and souls.

For example, we have an appetite for food, which is to be exercised within the boundaries of good nutrition and moderation. We have a desire for beauty, which is to be satisfied in purity. We have an appetite for sex, which is to be satisfied within the bounds of a marriage covenant. We have an appetite for sleep, which is to be met for the purposes of rejuvenation, not as an escape from life's responsibilities.

However, there are times when God asks us to set aside these natural appetites and concentrate on the spiritual dimension of our being. True fasting goes beyond skipping a meal or denying food for a period of time. It is a denial of all natural human appetites so we might concentrate solely on the Lord and what He wants to say to us. God may call us to a time of fasting and prayer to reveal an area of our lives that needs to be changed, to express His desires (and perhaps even a new direction for our lives), or to direct us to intercede for others.

The ultimate purpose for fasting and prayer rests with God. When we fast, submitting all of our normal life patterns to Him, He has our full attention and can mold us completely and totally for His purposes. When we are in this spiritual state, God can guide our prayers like arrows to accomplish His will. He can then do the real transforming work in our inner spirit that causes us to speak and act more like Jesus Christ.

**3.** "He changes the times and the seasons; He removes kings and raises up kings; He gives wisdom to the wise and knowledge to those who have understanding. He reveals deep and secret things" (Daniel 2:21-22). What sort of "deep and secret things" has the Lord revealed through prayer in your own life?

........................................................................................
........................................................................................
........................................................................................
........................................................................................
........................................................................................
........................................................................................

**4.** Why does God give wisdom to the wise, rather than to the foolish? Why does He give knowledge to those who have understanding, rather than to the ignorant?

........................................................................................
........................................................................................
........................................................................................
........................................................................................
........................................................................................
........................................................................................
........................................................................................

# INITIAL BENEFITS OF FASTING AND PRAYER

God's call to fasting and prayer is always for our benefit. The Bible points out at least seven benefits of fasting and prayer. *First, our attitudes and thoughts are pruned and purified so God might entrust us with a greater ministry.* By fasting and praying, we become more disciplined toward the things of the Father. We yield ourselves fully to Him. We give Him opportunity to cut away those things that will slow us down or keep us from the plans that He has for our lives.

Jesus fasted and prayed for forty days in the wilderness and was perfected for ministry (see Matthew 4:1–2, 11). Queen Esther fasted and prayed for three days and was stripped of the fear that kept her from telling the king about the plot against her people (see Esther 4:15–16). As we likewise confront the devil, using the Word of God as our weapon, we are made stronger. We know we have had a show-down with the enemy. We know the power of God's Word to defeat the enemy. We know that God is preparing us for His purposes.

*Second, we are able to discern more clearly the will of God for our lives.* Fasting clears our spiritual eyes and ears so we can discern what God desires to reveal. If you are facing a major decision, I strongly encour-age you to go away for three days of fasting and prayer. Spend your time in the Word of God. Rein in your attention so that you are to-tally focused on the things of God. Listen intently to what God de-sires to say to you. He will reveal what to do.

Daniel found this to be true. He was greatly troubled over the sin of Israel, but he set his face toward the God "to make request by prayer and supplications, with fasting, sackcloth, and ashes" (Daniel 9:3). While he was praying, the angel Gabriel came to him "to give [him] skill to understand' " (verse 22). God may not send an angel to tell you His will for your life, but He will give you under-standing. He will speak to your innermost spirit by the Holy Spirit concerning what action you are to take. He will reveal all you need to know so you can perform His will.

*Third, we are confronted with our sins so we might confess them to God, receive forgiveness, and walk in righteousness.* There may be an area in your life that you just can't change. Many times these habits are broken as you fast and pray. At other times, the Lord reveals something in your life that you need to confront and correct. You may not have been aware of it before, but as the Lord reveals it, you can respond immediately, "Lord, please forgive me of this and change me so I will not behave or think this way in the future." Fasting and prayer purify us as we face the temptations that have kept us entangled in sin.

**5.** "Then Jesus was led up by the Spirit into the wilderness to be tempted by the devil. And when He had fasted forty days and forty nights . . . the devil left Him, and behold, angels came and ministered to Him" (Matthew 4:1–2, 11). Why did Jesus fast for forty days? How might this have prepared Him for the temptations of the devil?

........................................................................................................

........................................................................................................

........................................................................................................

........................................................................................................

........................................................................................................

........................................................................................................

**6.** Note that Jesus' fasting did not drive away the devil. In fact, He was severely tempted while fasting. How did Jesus resist Satan? What does this teach about our fasting?

........................................................................................................

........................................................................................................

........................................................................................................

........................................................................................................

........................................................................................................

........................................................................................................

# FURTHER BENEFITS OF FASTING AND PRAYING

*A fourth benefit of fasting and prayers is that we experience a release of supernatural power in our lives.* The outcome of genuine fasting and prayer is spiritual growth, including a renewed outpouring of supernatural power. Furthermore, certain problems and situations cannot be resolved apart from fasting and prayer (see 2 Corinthians 10:4).

As Paul and Barnabas traveled in ministry, they made many disciples in Lystra, Iconium, and Antioch. They exhorted the disciples to continue in the faith, appointed elders in every church, "prayed with fasting," and "commended them to the Lord in whom they had believed" (Acts 14:22–23). The purpose of this prayer and fasting was to release supernatural power into the lives of the believers so that they might remain true to the Lord and endure any kind of tribulation. Likewise, prayer and fasting will strengthen us against the temptations of the enemy so we can endure any trouble that comes our way.

*Fifth, we can make an effect on national issues.* We have already noted how Jehoshaphat called the people of Israel to fasting and prayer. At the conclusion of Jehoshaphat's prayer, the Lord spoke through a prophet with the plan they were to follow. The battle plan was amazing—send out the choir before the soldiers (see 2 Chronicles 20:18–23). The plan worked, and it brought all the glory to God. As we fast and pray for our nation, God will move. He will pour out His Spirit, in His ways and in His timing. We can count on it.

*Sixth, we can help build up God's people.* Prayer is the generator of the church. It gives power to its ministers, propels outreach to the lost, and creates a climate in which evangelistic efforts succeed. Nehemiah heard about the plight of his people and the destruction of the walls of Jerusalem, and he "sat down and wept, and mourned for many days . . . fasting and praying before the God of heaven" (Nehemiah 1:4). As we hear of believers who are being persecuted, or are falling into sin, or are becoming lukewarm in the faith, we need to fast and pray that God will strengthen His people to withstand the enemy. God will answer our prayers.

*Seventh, our minds are sharpened.* When we fast and pray, our minds are quickened so we understand the Scriptures as never before. We are sensitive to God's timing and direction with an increased ability to discern. We are keenly aware of what God desires to accomplish in our lives and in the lives of others around us. When we fast and pray, the pollutants are removed so we can move freely in the flow of God's Holy Spirit.

**7.** "The weapons of our warfare are not carnal but mighty in God for pulling down strongholds, casting down arguments and every high thing that exalts itself against the knowledge of God, bringing every thought into captivity to the obedience of Christ" (2 Corinthians 10:4–5). What are "the weapons of our warfare"?

.................................................................................................................

.................................................................................................................

.................................................................................................................

.................................................................................................................

.................................................................................................................

.................................................................................................................

.................................................................................................................

**8.** What does it mean that our weapons "cast down arguments" and "bring every thought into captivity"? Give real-life examples.

.................................................................................................................

.................................................................................................................

.................................................................................................................

.................................................................................................................

.................................................................................................................

.................................................................................................................

.................................................................................................................

.................................................................................................................

## FOLLOW UP WITH ACTION

Fasting and prayer are to be followed up with action. In the story of Esther, she had to confront Haman in the presence of the king. In the book of Acts, we read how Cornelius—after fasting and praying—took the message of the gospel to the Gentiles (see Acts 10:30). The result of fasting in Paul's life was increased missionary service (see 2 Corinthians 6:5 and 11:27).

In the book of Isaiah, we read how God clearly called His people to action. The people asked God, "Why have we fasted . . . and You have not seen?" The Lord responded, "In fact, in the day of your fast you find pleasure, and exploit all your laborers. Indeed you fast for strife and debate, and to strike with the fist of wickedness" (58:3–4). God pointed out the people's motives were wrong and they were using fasting as a substitute for right action. He said, "Is this not the fast that I have chosen: to loose the bonds of wickedness, to undo the heavy burdens, to let the oppressed go free, and that you break every yoke?" (verse 6).

God will reveal through fasting and prayer something you are to *do*. It may be a change in a behavior or a call to a new behavior. Look for specific next-step actions that God has for you as you emerge from a time of fasting and prayer. He has a plan for you to fulfill.

9. What does it mean to "loose the bonds of wickedness," "undo heavy burdens," "let the oppressed go free," and "break every yoke"? Give practical examples.

10. How can prayer and fasting accomplish these things?

## TODAY AND TOMORROW

*Today:* Times of prayer and fasting help me clear
my spiritual vision and purify my life.

*Tomorrow:* I will ask the Lord to show me when He wants
me to spend time in fasting and prayer.

# CLOSING PRAYER

*Father, we thank You for giving us the examples of fasting and praying that
we find throughout the Scriptures. Help us to commit ourselves to begin
to fast, pray, and seek Your face. Move us to confess and repent of our sins
so that You may be able to use each and every one of us to our fullest potential.
We pray that together—in small groups, as the body of Christ, and as whole
nations—that through us You may demonstrate Your supernatural power.
We want the lost to know that You are alive, that You are God, that You are
sovereign, and that everything is under Your perfect control.*

# NOTES AND PRAYER REQUESTS

Use this space to write any key points, questions, or prayer requests from this week's study.

# A Prayer Burden

## IN THIS LESSON

*Learning:* What is a prayer burden?

*Growing:* What does God want me to do when
I feel burdened?

In the last lesson, we touched briefly on Nehemiah's response when he heard the walls of Jerusalem were broken and the gates of the city were burned. Nehemiah wrote, "I sat down and wept, and mourned for many days. . . . And I said: 'I pray, Lord God of heaven, O great and awesome God, You who keep Your covenant and mercy with those who love You and observe Your commandments, please let Your ear be attentive and Your eyes open, that You may hear the prayer of Your servant which I pray before You now, day and night'" (Nehemiah 1:4-6).

Nehemiah was experiencing a *prayer burden.* A prayer burden can be defined as a strong motivation to pray for others and carry the needs of others before God in prayer until God responds. The Bible has a great deal to say about such burdens. We are to bear one another's burdens (see Galatians 6:2). We are to go the second mile in helping another person (see Matthew 5:41). We are subject to God's punishment if we place burdens on others (see Amos 5:11 and Matthew 18:6-7).

Much of our ability to bear natural burdens is derived from developing our ability to carry spiritual burdens in prayer. A burden of prayer is marked usually by a sense of spiritual weight—a heaviness of heart, a spirit of mourning, or a feeling of restlessness that arises because we can't shift ourselves away from a problem that has come to our attention.

# THE SOURCE OF BURDENS

Burdens tend to arise from one of three sources. *First, a burden may be the result of a self-inflicted error, sin, or guilt.* This type of burden could be called a "burden of conviction." The Holy Spirit allows us to feel the full weight of our sin and guilt. The antidote for this type of burden is to confess our sin to God, receive His forgiveness, and move forward in our lives.

*Second, a burden may come from the negative behavior of another person.* We may find ourselves depressed under a load of guilt another person has laid on us or angry over another person's negative behavior. Our best response to this type of burden is to ask God to deal with the other person, to forgive us for anything we may have done (known or unknown), and to help us withstand the persecution. Jesus gave clear instructions about how to deal with those who persecute us. We are to have an attitude of love toward them, pray for them, speak well of them, and do good to them (see Matthew 5:44).

*Third, a prayer burden may come from God.* In these cases, God wants to get our attention about a matter so we will pray about it. The burden may be triggered by something somebody else says or does. In the Bible, we see how God used messengers from Jerusalem to tell Nehemiah about the brokenness of the Israelite people and the city. The burden to pray, however, came directly from God. The Lord was calling Nehemiah to focus on the problems at hand and to pray so that He could act.

God does not act in many situations because we do not pray. God gave us free will—which includes our ability to choose sin over righteousness—and will not override it. If you are burdened to pray for another person, God desires to act on that person's behalf. He places the burden to pray on your heart so that He has an opening in the spirit realm through which to move. As you pray, you are allowed to get in on the blessing that God has for you and for that person through an answered prayer. All prayer is thus threefold:

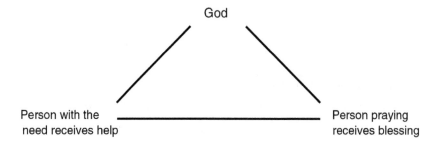

God

Person with the need receives help

Person praying receives blessing

This triangular aspect of prayer is the way God builds up His people to *be* a people, and not just isolated individuals who are in relationship with Him. God wants us to be in relationship with Him and in relationship with other people. The hallmark quality of this triangle is love. So, if God is burdening your heart, He is calling you to get involved in other people's problems and heartaches. This is part of God's teaching you how better to love others. In turn, God will place a burden on other people's hearts to pray for you.

1. "But I say to you, love your enemies, bless those who curse you, do good to those who hate you, and pray for those who spitefully use you and persecute you, that you may be sons of your Father

in heaven; for He makes His sun rise on the evil and on the good, and sends rain on the just and on the unjust" (Matthew 5:44–45). Why does Jesus say the Lord "makes His sun rise on the evil and on the good" in this context? What does this teach about prayer?

2. When have you prayed for someone who treated you badly? What resulted from those prayers—both in you and the other person?

# THE WEIGHT OF THE BURDEN

The weight of a prayer burden is determined by two things. *First, the burden is determined by the magnitude of the need.* A prayer burden may hit you with tremendous force, or it may be of lesser intensity but with a nagging persistence over several days and weeks. *Second, the weight of a burden is determined by how quickly God desires to deal with the situation.* Some problems are resolved immediately, others take time.

In either case, your response to a prayer burden must be immediate. You need to turn away from your daily routine and pray! Nehemiah's response was to sit down and weep as soon as he experienced his prayer burden. If God burdens your heart to pray about a matter, you may need to excuse yourself from the presence of others, change your schedule, or cancel an appointment. Don't let anything keep you away from prayer!

Let me warn you that the devil will launch every temptation to get you to stop praying and go on about your business. You will suddenly be reminded of a thousand "important" things that you need to do. The phone may ring repeatedly. You may feel guilt pangs because you are not doing your daily chores. If you have a burden to pray, however, the most important thing you can do before God is to obey Him and to pray.

Note that worry is different than feeling a burden. You know that you are experiencing worry when the focus of your concern is on *your* need or on how a particular problem affects *you*. Worry is always self-centered. A prayer burden is focused on God and what He wants to accomplish in the life of another person (or in the lives of a group of people).

If you don't know whether you are feeling worry or a prayer burden, ask God to reveal the nature of what you are experiencing. If your attention is directed to a particular person, God is calling you to pray for that person. However, if your attention is solely on yourself and how a problem might affect your life, you can know that is worry.

3. "Be sober, be vigilant; because your adversary the devil walks about like a roaring lion, seeking whom he may devour. Resist him, steadfast in the faith, knowing that the same sufferings are

experienced by your brotherhood in the world" (1 Peter 5:8–9). In practical terms, how does a Christian resist the devil?

.................................................................................................................

.................................................................................................................

.................................................................................................................

.................................................................................................................

.................................................................................................................

.................................................................................................................

.................................................................................................................

**4.** Why does Peter add that "the same sufferings" are being experienced by Christians around the world? What does this suggest about the spiritual battle?

.................................................................................................................

.................................................................................................................

.................................................................................................................

.................................................................................................................

.................................................................................................................

.................................................................................................................

.................................................................................................................

# THE DURATION OF A PRAYER BURDEN

The length of time that you experience a prayer burden is partly up to you. If you respond immediately to the burden to pray, God can begin to work through you more quickly. However, if you disobey God's prayer burden, it is likely to linger on until you obey.

Sometimes a prayer burden will rest on your heart for hours . . . and sometimes for months. Nehemiah's prayer burden lasted "many days." A prayer burden will last as long as it takes for you to hear clearly what God wants you to pray about. For this reason, when you experience a prayer burden, you must listen keenly for God to tell you what to pray for. A burden lifts when all of the preparation is completed so that God can act.

If the burden is related to a situation in your personal life, the process may take some time as God prepares you and changes you. If the burden is related to a situation in another person's life, then the burden is likely to last until you pray for precisely what God desires to do and until He has removed all obstacles from the path. This process may involve important interim changes in the life of another person or in the course of a circumstance. In Nehemiah's case, the burden lasted until he had prayed precisely for the things that God wanted to do and God had changed the heart of the Persian king.

Always keep in mind that God has good plans. Prayer is a good work performed on the behalf of others. It yields good results because God works all things for good to those who love Him (see Romans 8:28). A prayer burden is an invitation to be involved in a good process—one that yields a good harvest in your life and the lives of those for whom you are praying.

5. "And let us not grow weary while doing good, for in due season we shall reap if we do not lose heart" (Galatians 6:9). When have you found yourself growing weary while doing good? How did you find strength to continue?

**6.** In what ways might you be tempted to lose heart while praying? Where do you find strength to continue?

_____

_____

_____

_____

_____

_____

_____

## WHEN TO SHARE A PRAYER BURDEN

If God gives you a burden to pray for a specific person, you are to *pray* and not gossip about the person. You must not share the nature of the burden until you are free of any criticism related to the person for whom you are praying and until God gives you a green light to go to that person. Nobody else should be involved. The matter is between you, God, and the third party.

Some burdens, however, are collective in nature. For example, each of us should feel a strong burden to pray for the spiritual state of our nation as well as for individuals or groups of fellow believers who are facing trouble or a major challenge. In the book of Acts, we read how King Herod put the disciple James to death and then arrested Peter, intending to do the same to him. In response, "constant prayer was offered to God for him by the church" (12:5). The believers knew that their role in this matter was to seek God in prayer.

**7.** "Peter was sleeping, bound with two chains between two soldiers; and the guards before the door were keeping the prison. Now behold, an angel of the Lord stood by him, and a light shone in the prison; and he struck Peter on the side and raised him up, saying,

'Arise quickly!' And his chains fell off his hands" (Acts 12:6–7). How did God answer the believers' prayers for Peter's release?

.......................................................................

.......................................................................

.......................................................................

.......................................................................

.......................................................................

.......................................................................

.......................................................................

.......................................................................

**8.** What are some burdens that you have for your fellow believers in Christ? What steps are you taking to act on those burdens?

.......................................................................

.......................................................................

.......................................................................

.......................................................................

.......................................................................

.......................................................................

.......................................................................

.......................................................................

.......................................................................

.......................................................................

# THE RESULTS OF A PRAYER BURDEN

A prayer burden is one of God's methods of cleansing us. As we yield to His call to pray, we will become stripped of self-centeredness. As we pray, we will receive a blessing and have our faith renewed and strengthened. We will grow in our awareness of God's methods and plans. Ultimately, we will become a force for bringing about the victory of God over evil. We will become agents for good change and increased righteousness.

9. "If anyone wants to sue you and take away your tunic, let him have your cloak also. And whoever compels you to go one mile, go with him two" (Matthew 5:40–41). What are some practical examples from your life of what these verses are teaching?

10. If you give up both your cloak and tunic, how will you keep warm and clothed? What does God's Word say about this?

## TODAY AND TOMORROW

*Today:* The Lord gives us burdens to pray for others and for our own holiness.

*Tomorrow:* I will ask the Lord to show me specifically how to pray this week.

# CLOSING PRAYER

*Lord, thank You for calling us to a deeper level of communication with You through prayer. Thank You for impressing us with the need to focus all our attention—sometimes even through fasting—solely and completely on You. Don't spare us the burden. When You want to change a nation, place a heaviness on our hearts to seek You in prayer. Brighten the lights, stir the flame, and fan it into a fire that will compel us to not rest until Your will is done. We want to be a people who are willing to bear whatever burden You give and stay with it until we have secured the victory in Christ.*

# NOTES AND
# PRAYER REQUESTS

Use this space to write any key points, questions, or prayer requests from this week's study.

# GETTING ANSWERS TO PRAYER

## IN THIS LESSON

*Learning:* What must I do to get an answer from God?

*Growing:* Why doesn't God answer "yes" more often?

Many people think the only answered prayers are those that God answers with a *yes*. However, as we discussed in an earlier lesson, God sometimes answers us with *no* and *wait*. God's answers are always for our good, and they inevitably call us to grow in our faith and to walk more closely with Christ. Nevertheless, we want God to say *yes* in answer to our petitions.

We must recognize at the outset that God does not answer our prayers on the basis of our self-worth or our accomplishments. In other words, we cannot earn a *yes* answer from God. His answers are not granted on the basis of our being good in our own human nature. Rather, God's basis for answering our prayer is His love. If we ever doubt this, we need only to look to the cross. God sent His only Son, Jesus Christ, to die for our sins so that we might be restored to Him in loving fellowship and live with Him forever in heaven (see John 3:16).

God gives His children the desires of their hearts—if those desires are within the parameters of His will. If we delight in the things of God, we will desire to do God's will. God will quickly give us our desires because they are His own for our lives. When we ask something of God, He says *yes* to us if it will build us up, lead us to eternal life, and helps us to be more fruitful witnesses for Him on earth. He knows what is best for us. He will only give what is useful and beneficial for us and for those with whom we have a relationship.

Many people unfortunately think that God wants them to live in poverty. They deny their needs and shun possessions in an effort to increase their faith. The fact is, God delights in providing us what we need. We are to receive God's blessings with a spirit of gratitude. We may enjoy possessions, but we do not place our trust in them. Our loving heavenly Father does not want us to live with great areas of need in our lives. That brings no glory to Him.

At the other extreme are people who think that God should give them everything that they want at the snap of their fingers. The reality is that there are certain things that God does not grant to us for our good. If He granted all of our requests, we could easily become greedy and lose sight of His call for us to help others who are in need.

God balances His giving to us. He desires we walk in close relationship with Him, trusting Him to meet our needs and equip us in every area of our lives to do the work that He is calling us to do.

# A Right Relationship with God

In the Bible, God outlines five prerequisites for receiving *yes* answers to our prayers. *The first prerequisite is a right relationship with Him.* God wants us to live in fellowship with Him and others. Of course, at times we slip and cause our relationships with Him and others to be strained. We are human beings, and we have a great capacity to fail. God knows this.

He does not look at our track record nearly as much as He looks at our *motivation*. Is our aim and our desire to love and serve Him? If so, God will correct us and continue to hear our prayers and answer them with *yes*. Those who have a heart for God often fail and pick themselves up and try again, and fail and pick themselves up and try again. All the while, God knows they are desiring to move ever closer to Him and to serve Him to the best of their ability. Such people receive many *yes* answers to their prayers.

If our aim, however, is to continue willfully in sin and to ignore God's attempts at correcting us, then God is under no obligation to hear and answer us. We are choosing to pursue our own self-interests, which God knows inevitably will lead to our downfall. God will not contribute to anything that will be negative to our spiritual growth or cause pain to others.

1. "If I regard iniquity in my heart, the LORD will not hear. But certainly God has heard me; He has attended to the voice of my prayer" (Psalm 66:18–19). What do you think it means to "regard iniquity" in your heart? Why does God not hear your prayers in that condition?

......................................................................................

......................................................................................

......................................................................................

......................................................................................

......................................................................................

......................................................................................

......................................................................................

......................................................................................

......................................................................................

......................................................................................

......................................................................................

**2.** What is the solution to this situation (see 1 John 1:9)?

<br>
<br>
<br>
<br>
<br>
<br>
<br>

# A RIGHT METHOD

*A second prerequisite to receiving a yes answer from God is a right method.* God does not give us a universal formula for making our petitions, but He does ask us to be definite and specific in our prayers. He also tells us to ask with thanksgiving and with faith. Some people pray, "God, please bless the nation, bless the church, and bless my family." But what do they mean? How do they define *blessing*? Nobody would say to a waitress in a restaurant, "I want food and drink." When we order in a restaurant, we make a specific request.

I know people who say, "Well, God can read my mind and my heart. He knows what I want." My response to them is, "If you have a blank mind, what is God reading?" In the Bible, we read the story of an encounter between Jesus and a blind man named Bartimaeus. "When he heard that it was Jesus of Nazareth, he began to cry out and say, 'Jesus, Son of David, have mercy on me!'" (Mark 10:47). Jesus responded by asking, "What do you want Me to do for you?" (verse 51). Jesus asks the same question of us.

We are also to pray with thanksgiving. Our praise and thanksgiving to God are direct reflections of our faith—we are saying to God, "Lord, I know that You are working all things together for my good and You will grant me only what is for my eternal benefit. I thank You for giving me what I need, when I need it, and in the proper way. I am voicing my desires for what I believe is best for me, but I thank You for granting what You know to be the best for me."

**3.** "Be anxious for nothing, but in everything by prayer and supplication, with thanksgiving, let your requests be made known to God" (Philippians 4:6). Why does Paul say we should make our requests "with thanksgiving"? What are we to be thankful for?

.................................................................................................

.................................................................................................

.................................................................................................

.................................................................................................

.................................................................................................

.................................................................................................

.................................................................................................

.................................................................................................

.................................................................................................

.................................................................................................

**4.** What does anxiety have to do with prayer? Why are we commanded not to be anxious—how is our will involved in anxiety?

.................................................................................................

.................................................................................................

.................................................................................................

.................................................................................................

.................................................................................................

.................................................................................................

.................................................................................................

.................................................................................................

.................................................................................................

.................................................................................................

.................................................................................................

.................................................................................................

# A RIGHT REQUEST

*A third prerequisite to receiving a yes answer from God is a right request.*
If we desire to receive a *yes* answer from God, the request we make
must be according to His will (see 1 John 5:14). God has a plan and
a purpose for our lives. He sees precisely what will be involved and
required for that purpose to be fulfilled—today, tomorrow, next year,
and on down the path. He will not grant us a petition that causes
us to stray from that plan.

Jesus, on the night before His crucifixion, prayed in the Garden
of Gethsemane, "Not as I will, but as You will" (Matthew 26:39). Jesus
did not want to stray even one degree from God's perfect plan for His
life. His prayer must become our prayer, for then—and only then—can
we be assured of continual *yes* answers from the Lord.

God's plan for us includes His perfect timing. Some things may
be right for us . . . but not *right now*. When we pray, "Your will, not
mine," we must be aware we are also praying, "Your timing, not mine."

**5.** "[He] prayed, saying, 'O My Father, if it is possible, let this cup
pass from Me; nevertheless, not as I will, but as You will' (Matthew 26: 39). What were Jesus' desires in this passage? How important were these things to Him?

**6.** What desire was greatest in His mind? What price was He willing to pay to attain that goal?

..................................................................................................

..................................................................................................

..................................................................................................

..................................................................................................

..................................................................................................

..................................................................................................

..................................................................................................

# A RIGHT FRAMEWORK

*A fourth prerequisite to receiving a yes answer from God is a right framework.* There is no formula for prayer, but there is a framework. Our prayers are to be voiced in the name of Jesus.

Many people close all of their prayers with the phrase, "in the name of Jesus, amen." Some do this as if this phrase is a magic tag to get what they want. Nothing could be farther from the truth of God. Others take God's promises regarding the name of Jesus to mean they can ask for anything they want and then seal it with the name of Jesus to ensure they get it. They look for a particular promise in the Bible and then claim it "in the name of Jesus" for themselves. They are asking amiss. The emphasis must always be on abiding fully in the name of Jesus and not on the request that we make.

To pray in the name of Jesus means to pray as if Jesus Himself were voicing the prayer. To be "in His name" is to have His identity so buried in our own that we are totally covered with Christ. To any observer in the heavenly realm, we are operating as if Christ Himself were acting or speaking. What we ask in Jesus' name must be completely in character with what Jesus would ask if He were walking in our shoes. What would Jesus need? What would Jesus desire?

These are the things that we are to request in Jesus' name. When we do, we are in the proper position to receive a *yes* answer from God.

**7.** "You did not choose Me, but I chose you and appointed you that you should go and bear fruit, and that your fruit should remain, that whatever you ask the Father in My name He may give you" (John 15:16). What sort of "fruit" does God want you to bear? How will such fruit "remain"?

**8.** In what way is fruit-bearing a prerequisite for answered prayers? In what way is answered prayer *not* a result of good works?

# A RIGHT ATTITUDE

*A fifth and final prerequisite to receiving a yes answer from God is a right attitude.* We are always to make our petitions without doubt. Our attitude must be one of faith. As James writes, "If any of you lacks wisdom, let him ask of God, who gives to all liberally and without reproach, and it will be given to him. But let him ask in faith, with no doubting, for he who doubts is like a wave of the sea driven and tossed by the wind" (James 1:5–6).

Many people ask God for things, but the tone of their voice conveys, "Oh, but I'm not worthy of this." Perhaps they are attempting to be humble, but if so, they are displaying a false humility. God calls us to make our petitions boldly, in faith, and without doubt. We base our faith on the fact that God wants only what is best for us. So, if we ask for what God desires for us, we must ask as if we are already in the process of receiving it.

You may say, "But what if I am asking for the wrong thing?" The Lord will show you if you are asking for something in error. You are not omniscient—and God doesn't expect you to be. What He does expect of you is that you exercise faith and keep an open heart for Him to guide you into the *precision of perfection* that He desires for you.

If you come to Him with that attitude, He will grant you many yes answers, and He will lead you to ask only for those things that He can answer with a yes.

9. "Let him ask in faith, with no doubting, for he who doubts is like a wave of the sea driven and tossed by the wind" (James 1:6). Picture a wind-tossed wave in your mind. How is that a picture of someone asking for wisdom without faith?

**10.** When have you asked God for wisdom in a difficult situation? What was the result?

_____

_____

_____

_____

_____

_____

_____

_____

_____

_____

## ALL FOR GOD'S GLORY

When we voice our prayers out of a right relationship with God and in a specific and thankful way, we can be assured that we are praying in Jesus' name and that our requests will be in keeping with God's will. Each of the five prerequisites to _yes_ answers works together with all of the others. For example, a right attitude flows from a right relationship. A right request is best voiced with the right method. The right framework is directly linked to a right relationship.

The reason God says _yes_ to our prayers is so we might find fulfillment and joy and so that He might be glorified. Jesus said, "Let your light so shine before men, that they may see your good works and glorify your Father in heaven" (Matthew 5:16). When nonbelievers see us living in right relationship with God and the Lord answering our prayers, they are drawn to Him. They desire to know Him as their Lord. God wants to say _yes_ to you when you pray.

## TODAY AND TOMORROW

*Today:* God wants to say *yes* to my prayer requests because He wants me to be like Jesus.

*Tomorrow:* I will ask the Lord to teach me how to pray in His will this week.

# CLOSING PRAYER

*Lord, thank You for giving Your children the desires of their hearts—when those desires fall within the parameters of Your will. Teach us today to take delight in the things in which you take delight. We want our purposes and our motivations to line up with Your will and to be fruitful for Your kingdom. We want to stand in right relationship with You. We want to employ the right method, make the right requests, and have the right framework and attitude in our prayers. Reveal to us any areas in our lives that are lacking—areas where we are not seeing prayers answered because our requests to do not line up with Your perfect purposes.*

# Notes and Prayer Requests

Use this space to write any key points, questions, or prayer requests from this week's study.

# Praying in the Will of God

*Learning:* What does it mean to pray in the will of God?

*Growing:* How can I find God's will for my life?

In the last lesson, we touched on the necessity for us to pray according to God's will. However, many of us struggle with knowing God's will. We have no difficulty with the big picture—we accept Jesus as Savior and keep His commandments—but struggle with how to make daily decisions regarding our families, jobs, church commitments, and friendships. In other words, we know how to pray about the *eternal* issues but are unsure about daily, practical matters.

The disciple John wrote, "Now this is the confidence that we have in Him, that if we ask anything according to His will, He hears us. And if we know that He hears us, whatever we ask, we know that we have the petitions that we have asked of Him (1 John 5:14–15).

These verses bear a threefold promise to us: (1) God hears us when we pray according to His will, (2) we will possess what we request if we ask according to His will, and (3) we will know that we will possess what we ask if we ask according to His will.

When we have the confidence of knowing that God is granting our petitions, we have a great boldness and freedom. Note that these verses also deal with our personal requests. Some believe they are being proud or presumptuous in asking God to meet their needs, but that opinion is not Scriptural. God wants you always to ask for the things that you want and need.

## GOD WANTS US TO KNOW

John assures us that believers in Christ can pray about *anything*. No issue is too big or too small to bring to God in prayer. His words also convey to us the truth that we *can* know the will of God. After all, if it were impossible for us to know the will of God, these verses would be null and void. But to the contrary, they encourage us to seek God's will and to live within it. The will of God is what is *pleasing to God* and *according to God's purposes*.

We cannot know everything that God purposes, because God's ways are higher than our ways (see Isaiah 55:8–9). God is omniscient and eternal. He knows all things, has plans and purposes, and is operating on a timetable that we can never know fully. However, *we can know God's purposes for us to the degree that He wants us to know*. We can count on God to reveal all the information that we need to defeat the devil and fulfill God's plan for our lives.

We cannot know all of God's purposes, but we can know the ones that involve us. In other words, we can know if we should marry a certain person, buy a certain car, take a certain job, or make other decisions that directly involve us. Furthermore, if we don't know how to pray about a specific situation, we can trust the Holy Spirit to guide our prayers so that we will know the mind of God, even as the Spirit knows the mind of God (see Romans 8:26–27). God wants us to have spiritual understanding and practical wisdom.

1. "Likewise the Spirit also helps in our weaknesses. For we do not know what we should pray for as we ought, but the Spirit Himself makes intercession for us with groanings which cannot be uttered" (Romans 8:26). What weaknesses does the Holy Spirit help you with? What do these weaknesses have to do with prayer?

........................................................................................................

........................................................................................................

........................................................................................................

........................................................................................................

........................................................................................................

........................................................................................................

........................................................................................................

2. Why does the Holy Spirit intercede for you with "groanings which cannot be uttered"? How is that a comforting thought when you don't know how to pray?

........................................................................................................

........................................................................................................

........................................................................................................

........................................................................................................

........................................................................................................

........................................................................................................

# IMPROPER APPROACHES TO KNOWING GOD'S WILL

Sometimes when people pray, "Lord, if it is Your will," they do so because they don't want to take the time or make the effort to actually know God's will. They often use Jesus' words, "Nevertheless, not as I will, but as You will" (Matthew 26:39), to justify their approach.

However, what they wrongly assume from these verses is that Jesus did not know God's will, which is why He prayed, "Your will be done." Some people even believe that Jesus really did not want to do God's will and die on the cross. He therefore was asking God to change His mind, but He was willing to accept God's purpose for His life if God did not change His mind.

This is not what these verses are saying. Jesus knew that He had to die on the cross. The "cup" to which he referred was not the cross. He had told His disciples about His death repeatedly as they made their plans to come to Jerusalem in the weeks before His crucifixion. He made it clear that He had to suffer at the hands of the religious leadership, be crucified, and rise again the third day. He knew clearly that God's purpose for Him was to die a sacrificial death at precisely the right time so that all of the Scriptures would be fulfilled concerning the "Lamb slain from the foundation of the world" (see Revelation 13:8). He knew He had to die in Jerusalem at the time of Passover.

So, to what "cup" was Jesus referring? Jesus knew that when He bore the sin of the world on the cross, He and the Father would be separated for a period of time, because the Father could not look on sin. To be separated from the Father—even for a fraction of a second—was unthinkable for Jesus. He had never been separated from the Father for even one moment in all of eternity up to that point. His request of God was that if there were any way this aspect of the cross might be altered . . . He wanted it to be altered.

God wants us to know His will and to pray within His will. We are not to pray for anything that pops into our minds and then tack on the statement, "if it is Your will," assuming that we will get what we wish for if it is God's will. This kind of prayer signifies an immature relationship with the heavenly Father. God desires, rather, that our relationship with Him be so personal and intimate that we know His will and are bold to claim it.

Some of us also seek to determine God's will by "throwing fleeces." We take the attitude, "If X happens, then I will do one thing . . . but if *Y* happens, I will do another." The practice comes from the book of Judges, where we read that God called Gideon to engage in battle with the Midianites. Gideon responded by asking God to perform three tests with a fleece of wool to confirm His word (see Judges 6:36–40).

I want to point out three things about this story. First, the fleece-throwing was Gideon's idea. Nowhere in Scripture does God authorize this as a desirable method for knowing His purposes. Second, this is the only time in the Bible when the method is used. Third, Gideon did not pose the tests to God to know His will but to gain confidence in the outcome that God had promised. Gideon already knew it was God's will for him to lead the people into battle. The armies had already been gathered for that battle. Gideon knew he was the leader. He was asking God for a sign that he and the Israelites were going to be successful.

Repeatedly in the Bible, God calls us to be faithful to Him without regard to whether we will be successful. True trust in God is to follow Him wherever He leads and do whatever He directs without concern for the outcome. Gideon's fleece-throwing was a sign that he didn't trust God. Fleece-throwing is used by people who don't really trust God to be true to His word.

**3.** Have you ever looked for a special sign concerning God's leading? If so, what type of fears were motivating your requests?

**4.** When have you stepped out boldly in faith to obey God's leading, without being guaranteed success? What was the outcome of that act of faith?

........................................................................................

........................................................................................

........................................................................................

........................................................................................

........................................................................................

........................................................................................

........................................................................................

........................................................................................

........................................................................................

# DISTINGUISH DESIRE, NEED, AND OPPORTUNITY

Throughout this study, I am assuming that you are in a right relationship with God as you approach Him in prayer. A right relationship with God is imperative for you to discern His will. If you have not accepted Jesus as your Savior, you do not have the Holy Spirit to guide your prayers and prompt you in right directions. If you are in willful disobedience to God, the foremost will of God is that you confess your disobedience, repent, receive His forgiveness, and obey Him. All other requests are subject to your willingness to obey and do what God reveals.

On the other hand, if you are in right relationship with God, you are likely to find the following threefold approach to be useful as you seek God's will. *The first step in this approach is to distinguish between need, desire, and opportunity.* What circumstance are you facing and how do they make you feel? Do you need a specific amount of money? Then you have a need. Do you have a longing to be married to a particular person? Then you have a desire. Are you being approached about a change in employment? Then you are facing opportunity.

The Bible clearly states that God wants to help you with your needs, desires, and decisions regarding opportunities. As David wrote, "May He grant you according to your heart's desire, and fulfill all your purpose" (Psalm 20:4). So steep yourself in the verses in the Bible that promise you His continual help and provision.

5. "Trust in the LORD, and do good; dwell in the land, and feed on His faithfulness. Delight yourself also in the LORD, and He shall give you the desires of your heart. Commit your way to the LORD, trust also in Him, and He shall bring it to pass" (Psalm 37:3–5). What things are precursors to receiving what you want from God?

6. What does it mean to "feed on God's faithfulness"? How is this done in practical terms?

# FIND A BIBLICAL EXAMPLE

*A second practical step to determining God's will is to find a biblical example.*
Ask God to reveal a passage of Scripture that addresses your situation. The Bible is filled with examples that cover the entire range of human need, desires, and opportunities. You may come across such an example as part of your daily reading of God's Word, or you may need to engage in a Bible study, using a concordance and searching the Scriptures until you find biblical examples.

Once you have a Scripture example, don't read just one verse and then say, "Great, here is my answer." Rather, meditate on the entire passage of Scripture that pertains to your situation. This is critically important, because the meditation process is a sifting and refining process. Ponder what God is saying and relate that truth to other areas of His Word. Take some time to *know* what God is saying and specifically what He seems to be saying to you.

Then go to God in prayer. Say, "Lord, I trust You to give me Your wisdom according to James 1:5. I trust the Holy Spirit will help me pray as I should pray according to Romans 8:26–27. I have found these examples in Your Word that relate to my situation. I want to do Your will, and I submit myself to You. On the basis of Your Word and my desire to follow You, I'm coming to You right now with this particular need [or desire or opportunity], and I am asking You to meet my need [answer my desire, or help me make a choice regarding this opportunity]."

Pray with faith! Thank God for giving you His wisdom and answering your prayer. Believe you have His full assurance that you will know His will and that He is going to grant your petition. Claim this is going to be done in God's timing . . . and start thanking Him for doing it. You don't need to know all the details about how and when God is going to act. Start thanking Him now for giving you the assurance that He is going to meet your need, guide you in your desire, or help you in responding to an opportunity.

**7.** What are some passages of Scripture that have been especially helpful to you as you have sought to find God's will? How have those passages helped you?

.................................................................................................

.................................................................................................

.................................................................................................

.................................................................................................

.................................................................................................

**8.** Recall an experience in your life in which you felt a close kinship with what a Bible character was thinking or feeling. What confidence did you draw from that example?

.................................................................................................

.................................................................................................

.................................................................................................

.................................................................................................

.................................................................................................

# ASK GOD TO REVEAL THE PATH

*A third practical step to determining God's will is to simply ask the Lord to reveal the path you should take.* If you are facing two equally good choices, ask God to reveal which one to take. Again, find a passage in the Bible that relates to your situation. Claim God's guidance for your life and then pray, "Show me what to choose. I will obey You fully as You reveal what to do."

Often when you pray this way, God will reveal another way that is the perfect path. Sometimes He will make it clear that He favors one particular way. Other times He will leave the choice up to you. Either way is acceptable to Him as part of His will, and He gives you the free reign to choose which one to take.

The key is to *wait* until you know with certainty how God wants you to respond. This is important, as you will likely come to a fuller understanding of the situation as you wait. As you meditate about the situation in prayer over several hours or days, and consider carefully what the Spirit is speaking in your heart, you will gain clarity about all aspects of the decision you are making. Don't rush to a decision until you know with certainty that you have heard from God.

God's perfect plan for your life will envelop you in peace. You will have a feeling of resolution in your heart. You will feel great peace of mind. When you feel unsettled or troubled about the decision you have made after following this Bible-based process, you can know that you are not experiencing God's direction. Knowing His will allows you to move calmly and with confidence—even in desperate situations or in the face of enormous challenges.

9. "Trust in the LORD with all your heart, and lean not on your own understanding; in all your ways acknowledge Him, and He shall direct your paths" (Proverbs 3:5–6). What does it mean to acknowledge God in all your ways? How is this done?

10. How will acknowledging God in all your ways influence your prayers? How will it influence your understanding of God's will for your life?

## TODAY AND TOMORROW

*Today:* The Lord wants me to understand His will even more than I want it—I just have to ask.

*Tomorrow:* I will spend time meditating on Scripture this week, asking the Lord to reveal His will to me.

# CLOSING PRAYER

*Lord God, we have no greater privilege than bowing our heads, hearts, and spirits before You—our omnipotent, holy, loving, gracious, generous, and kind heavenly Father. We know in our hearts that You want to answer our prayers. Instruct us as to how we should make our petitions to You. Grant us the desire to want to know Your will in every given situation. For You have promised that if we wait on You, You will clear up all the anxiety and show us exactly how to pray. Give us the assurance that when we come to You, we should come expecting—clearly anticipating—that You will answer our request, for we are asking according to Your perfect will.*

# NOTES AND
# PRAYER REQUESTS

Use this space to write any key points, questions, or prayer requests from this week's study.

# WHY PRAYERS AREN'T ANSWERED

## IN THIS LESSON

*Learning:* Why does God keep saying *no* to my prayers?

*Growing:* Why am I always waiting for an answer?

In this lesson, we will focus on God's *wait* and *no* answers to see what they might tell us. Again, I am assuming you are in right relationship with God. The person who has not accepted Jesus Christ as Savior or is in willful rebellion against God cannot expect *yes* answers from God. The Lord's answer is likely to be a repeated *no* until the person surrenders his or her life fully to Christ. Being a believer, however, and even desiring to live in right relationship with God, does not always ensure that we will have all of our prayers answered with a *yes*. There are certain practical and specific reasons why God doesn't always say *yes* even to Christians.

# Reasons for God's *Wait* Answer

God wants us to desire Him more than any person, position, or object. He wants us to trust Him completely to meet our needs and for us to be in an intimate relationship with Him. For this reason, *sometimes God answers wait so we will refocus on Him and not on the object of our desire.* God wants us to see Him as the source of our supply and know that a relationship with Him is far more valuable than any answered prayer could ever be.

*Sometimes, God answers wait so that we might trust Him more fully.* If God immediately said *yes* to all of our prayers, we might soon think that His answers were based on our own righteousness rather than on His mercy and grace. In giving us *wait* answers, God is building a stronger foundation of faith in us—one that will endure all persecutions and trials.

*Sometimes, God answers wait so our attitude will reflect the attitude of Christ.* God may want us to have a different attitude so we will know how to use the blessing that He is about to give us. At other times, we must mature in some way so we can handle the blessing. A young child may want a pocketknife, but a wise parent knows this is not an appropriate gift for a young child. The parent waits until the child is older and can use the pocketknife properly. Likewise, God may delay His answer to our prayer until we are better prepared to accept it.

*Sometimes, God answers wait because certain aspects of His plan are not fulfilled.* Other people may be involved in the blessing, and God may need to work in their hearts before He can give us what He wants us to have. He needs to remove the hindrances that keep His will from being enacted. To *hinder* literally means to break up, or to place an obstacle in the road, so that our way is impeded. God may need to do some "removal work" in the heart of another person before that person can share in our blessing.

*Finally, God sometimes answers wait because He is preparing for an even greater blessing than the one for which we asked.* This certainly was true in the case of Lazarus. Jesus knew that Lazarus was ill, and He could have gone to him to heal him before he died. Instead, Jesus waited until Lazarus had died so that He might raise him from the dead as a definitive sign of His authority over death (see John 11:1–45).

1. "You will keep him in perfect peace, whose mind is stayed on You, because he trusts in You" (Isaiah 26:3). What does it mean to have your mind "stayed on" God? How is this accomplished?

........................................................................................

........................................................................................

........................................................................................

........................................................................................

........................................................................................

........................................................................................

........................................................................................

2. When have you experienced the peace of God in the midst of trouble? What does this suggest about the promise in this verse?

........................................................................................

........................................................................................

........................................................................................

........................................................................................

........................................................................................

........................................................................................

........................................................................................

# A *NO* ANSWER DUE TO RELATIONSHIP ISSUES

When we hear about someone receiving an answer of *no* from God, our first impulse may be to assume there is sin in that person's life. Likewise, when we are the ones receiving the *no* answer, we may assume sin is the cause and try to argue that point with God or justify our position. The greater reality, however, is that we probably are in *error*, not sin, and God is using a *no* answer to correct our error.

Sin is willful disobedience against what we know God wants. Sin is a matter of saying, "I know what God's commandments say, but I choose to do otherwise." It is a deliberate act of rebellion and defiance. We experience a breach in our relationship with God, and the Holy Spirit moves to convict us of our sin. Error, in contrast, is an inadvertent disobedience. We do not know we are making an incorrect choice or engaging in unrighteous behavior because we have not been taught what we are doing is wrong. We desire a relationship with God and are quick to amend our ways once we realize our error, but at present we do not know we are erring.

God's answer of *no* is a means of bringing us to the point where we recognize our error so we can correct our behavior. Once we do, God's answer to our same petition may very well be *yes*. There are at least six areas of error that evoke such a *no* answer from God.

*First, God may answer no if our relationships with others are not right.* Our heavenly Father will not answer our prayers as long as we remain unforgiving, unmerciful, or self-centered toward family members and friends. We cannot be caustic, resentful, or selfish to other people and expect God to answer our petitions. He has clearly stated that we must forgive if we are to be forgiven. We must be givers before we expect to receive (see Luke 6:37–38).

In 1 Peter 3:1–7, we find a balanced approach to the relationship that God wants a husband and wife to have. Peter says that if this relationship is not in right balance, our prayers are hindered. Your relationship must be right with your spouse for God to answer your prayers, because in marriage, two people are made one and are regarded as one flesh by God (see Mark 10:6–8). Your request to God must be one that honors and considers your spouse.

3. "For if you forgive men their trespasses, your heavenly Father will also forgive you. But if you do not forgive men their trespasses,

neither will your Father forgive your trespasses" (Matthew 6:14–15). How does Jesus stress the importance of having right relationships? What is required of you to receive a *yes* answer from God?

.................................................................................................

.................................................................................................

.................................................................................................

.................................................................................................

.................................................................................................

.................................................................................................

.................................................................................................

**4.** "Therefore if you bring your gift to the altar, and there remember that your brother has something against you, leave your gift there before the altar, and go your way. First be reconciled to your brother, and then come and offer your gift" (Matthew 5:23–24). What does this say about the priority God places on forgiveness and reconciliation?

.................................................................................................

.................................................................................................

.................................................................................................

.................................................................................................

.................................................................................................

.................................................................................................

.................................................................................................

## A *NO* ANSWER DUE TO SELF-CENTEREDNESS

*A second reason God may answer no is because our motives are for self alone.* As James writes, "You ask and do not receive, because you ask amiss, that you may spend it on your pleasures" (James 4:3). All of our actions are either aimed at self or at God. Our motive is either to exalt ourselves or to bring glory to God. In serving others, we bring glory to God. So, we might say that our actions are motivated either by a desire to serve self or others.

God may give us a *no* answer so we can confront our own motives. Why are we asking God for a certain thing? Is it so we will look better, feel better, or get more praise from other people? Or is it so we might help others and be better able to fulfill the destiny that God has laid before us? God will not answer our prayers unless He is certain that we will be good stewards of the things He gives to us and be generous to others.

Specifically, God expects us to be generous to those who are in need. Many of God's blessings in the Bible are reserved for those who take care of the poor, the widows, and the orphans. We must use what God gives us to bring about justice and equity for those who are lacking the basic essentials of life.

5. "You lust and do not have. You murder and covet and cannot obtain. You fight and war. Yet you do not have because you do not ask. You ask and do not receive, because you ask amiss, that you may spend it on your pleasures" (James 4:2–3). What is the reason some people don't ask God for what they need? How do they try to get their desires?

**6.** What does it mean to "spend [what you receive] on your pleasures"? How is that motivation similar to those who "lust and do not have" in the first place?

........................................................................

........................................................................

........................................................................

........................................................................

........................................................................

........................................................................

........................................................................

# A *No* Answer Due to Wavering Faith or Failure to Tithe

*A third reason God may answer no is because we are wishy-washy in our faith.* God has little regard for faith that wavers—a faith that says, "Maybe God will . . . but maybe He won't." Such faith is unstable and unreliable. For this reason, God sometimes gives us an answer of *no* so we will reevaluate our opinion of God and come to grips with our own emotions.

Many people today are driven by their emotions. One day they claim to feel God's presence and they have joy and peace. The next day, when they are a little down or discouraged, they say they don't feel God's presence and therefore God must not care about them. They become resentful and bitter toward Him. God, however, hasn't changed. Their emotional temperament is being tossed about like wind-driven waves. Our relationship with God must be based on what the Bible says, not on how we feel on any given day. Feelings come and go, but God's Word remains. Our prayers must be grounded in the Word, not in ourselves.

*A fourth reason God may answer no is due to a failure to tithe.* God does not tolerate stinginess—whether toward Him or other people. If God does not seem to be answering your request for things, money, or material goods, check your giving. It may be that God is seeking to teach you a new set of priorities in your handling of money. He may be attempting to give you a new understanding of stewardship. God will not violate the cycle of giving that He established for mankind: giving, receiving, giving, receiving. His law requires reciprocity.

7. "But let him ask in faith, with no doubting, for he who doubts is like a wave of the sea driven and tossed by the wind. For let not that man suppose that he will receive anything from the Lord" (James 1:6–7). What does this passage say about praying in faith? Why do you think God requires you to not doubt when you pray?

8. "'Bring all the tithes into the storehouse, that there may be food in My house, and try Me now in this,' Says the Lord of hosts, 'If I will not open for you the windows of heaven and pour out for you such blessing that there will not be room enough to receive it'" (Malachi 3:10). What is the promise in this verse for those who are generous?

# A *No* Answer Due to Indifference to God's Word and Unconfessed Sin

*A fifth reason God may answer no is because we are indifferent to His Word.* Sometimes God gives us an answer of *no* so we will get serious about reading His Word and applying it to our lives. We cannot live with a closed Bible and expect to have an open line to heaven. The Bible is God's manual for right living. It contains His promises related to prayer and holds His commandments for how to receive His blessings and defeat the enemy of our souls.

We cannot turn a deaf ear to God's Word and then approach God with our requests. This would be like a college student telling his professors, "I don't need to attend classes or study any courses. Just give me a degree and I'll be on my way." The Bible has both information and inspiration that we need for our daily walk with God. So avail yourself of it. You will gain important insights into how to pray so that you get *yes* answers from God.

*Finally, we may receive and answer of no from God because we have unconfessed sins.* Just recognizing our sins is not enough—we must confess them to God and receive His forgiveness. God cannot give us *yes* answers if we only recognize our errors but do not obey Him and change our ways.

God's foremost desire is not to give us answers of *wait* or *no* but to say *yes* to us. As Moses said to the people, "Now it shall come to pass, if you diligently obey the voice of the Lord your God, to observe carefully all His commandments which I command you today, that the Lord your God will set you high above all nations of the earth. And all these blessings shall come upon you and overtake you, because you obey the voice of the Lord your God" (Deuteronomy 28:1–2).

God's desire is for blessing, but if you turn to follow other gods and do not obey His Word, you will find the "heavens which are over your head shall be bronze, and the earth which is under you shall be iron" (verse 23). In other words, the heavens will be closed to your prayers, and nothing you attempt to do will prosper. When you know what to do, you are responsible for doing it. Only then can God trust you with His *yes* answers and His blessings.

**9.** "One who turns away his ear from hearing the law, even his prayer is an abomination" (Proverbs 28:9). Why would God consider a person's prayer "an abomination" if that person turned a deaf ear to His law? What does this principle teach about unconfessed sin? What does it teach about reading God's Word?

**10.** "But your iniquities have separated you from your God; and your sins have hidden His face from you, so that He will not hear" (Isaiah 59:2). Is there unconfessed sin in your life at present? If so, stop right now and spend time confessing it to the Lord.

## TODAY AND TOMORROW

*Today:* The Lord sometimes says *no* or *wait* because
it is best for me.

*Tomorrow:* I will ask God to show me anything in my
life that is hindering my prayers this week.

# CLOSING PRAYER

*Father, we take so many things for granted. We treat You like we treat each other—like others treat us. We rationalize so many things. We excuse so many things. We overlook our own failings and then wonder why the heavens seem to be like brass when we pray. We know that You love to answer our prayers— but that You will never violate Your own laws to give us something that will end up being a detriment to us. Help us to be honest enough to examine our lives, confess our sins, and move into the state of righteousness that You desire for us.*

# NOTES AND PRAYER REQUESTS

· · · · · · · · · · · · · · · · · · · · · · · · · · · · · · · · · · · · · · · · · ·

Use this space to write any key points, questions, or prayer requests
from this week's study.

# PRAYING FOR OTHERS

## IN THIS LESSON

*Learning:* Why should I pray for the needs of others?

*Growing:* What is the best way to pray for someone whom I don't know well?

The Bible calls us to a life of prayer that includes praying for others. As the apostle Paul told Timothy:

> Therefore I exhort first of all that supplications, prayers, intercessions, and giving of thanks be made for all men, for kings and all who are in authority, that we may lead a quiet and peaceable life in all godliness and reverence. For this is good and acceptable in the sight of God our Savior, who desires all men to be saved and to come to the knowledge of the truth. . . . I desire therefore that the men pray everywhere, lifting up holy hands, without wrath and doubting" (1 Timothy 2:1–4, 8).

There are a few keys points to take away from this passage.

# Praying for Those in Authority, the Lost, and the Church

*First, this passage reveals we should pray for those who have authority over us.* This includes political leaders, as well as judicial, social, and economic leaders. We should pray that our leaders have a strong reverence for God and His commandments. We need leaders who will openly acknowledge the sovereignty of God. Only then will they make decisions, pass laws, and give legal opinions that allow Christians to live in peace and share the gospel.

*Second, we should pray for those who do not know the Lord.* We have a commission from God throughout the Bible to pray for the lost. Jesus said to His disciples, "The harvest truly is plentiful, but the laborers are few. Therefore pray the Lord of the harvest to send out laborers into His harvest" (Matthew 9:37–38). If we are to see the lost come to Christ, we must pray for them and pray for laborers to be sent to them.

Can you imagine what a different world we would live in if the majority of any community had an understanding of the truth and came to know the Lord? The crime rate would decrease, cooperative efforts for good would abound, drug and alcohol use would diminish, businesses would become more productive, neighborhoods would be friendlier—the list of benefits is virtually endless!

*Third, we should pray for the body of Christ.* We need to be praying for believers who are being persecuted, those who are lukewarm in their faith, those who are in rebellion against God, and those who are in need. Paul persistently prayed for those in the churches that he helped to establish. As he wrote in his letter to the Colossians, "We give thanks to the God and Father of our Lord Jesus Christ, praying always for you, since we heard of your faith in Christ Jesus and of your love for all the saints. . . . We also, since the day we heard [the news of your faith], do not cease to pray for you" (Colossians 1:3–4, 9).

Paul continued by providing a clear outline for how we are to pray for our fellow believers. He begins by asking God to fill the congregation with the knowledge of His will in all wisdom and spiritual understanding (see verse 9). He prayed they would walk worthy of the Lord, being fruitful in every good work, and increase in their knowledge of God (see verse 10). He requested that God would strengthen them with all might, according to His glorious power, and given them all patience and longsuffering, with joy (see verse 11). Finally, Paul gave thanks to the Father for them, whom he said had qualified them to be partakers of the inheritance of the saints in the light (see verse 12).

**1.** What does it mean to "walk worthy of the Lord"? How is this done in practical terms?

........................................................................................................

........................................................................................................

........................................................................................................

........................................................................................................

........................................................................................................

........................................................................................................

........................................................................................................

........................................................................................................

........................................................................................................

**2.** Do you pray regularly for other people? Are other people praying regularly for you?

........................................................................................................

........................................................................................................

........................................................................................................

........................................................................................................

........................................................................................................

........................................................................................................

........................................................................................................

........................................................................................................

........................................................................................................

# PRAYING FOR OUR LEADERS
# AND THOSE WHO PERSECUTE US

*Fourth, we should pray for our pastors and ministry leaders.* In Ephesians, Paul asked the church to pray for him "that utterance may be given to me, that I may open my mouth boldly to make known the mystery of the gospel" (6:19). We are to pray that God will show our leaders what to say, give them boldness to say it, and help them to speak with clarity so that the gospel is no longer a mystery. We also must pray that our church leaders will stay faithful to the Lord, keep His commandments, and be given strength to withstand the assaults of the devil.

*We are also to pray for those who persecute us.* Jesus taught how we are to deal with our enemies: "Love your enemies, bless those who curse you, do good to those who hate you, and pray for those who spitefully use you and persecute you, that you may be sons of your Father in heaven" (Matthew 5:44–45). As long as we harbor hatred, bitterness, and resentment toward our enemies, we are not trusting the Lord to deal with them as *He* wills. However, when we pray for our enemies with an attitude of forgiveness and love, God is free to deal with them with His omniscient and omnipotent love. He can cleanse their hearts. He can heal them and make them whole. Of course, this includes their having a good relationship with us.

The benefit of all these prayers, the Bible says, is that we may be allowed to live Christian lives that will flourish, prosper, and be fulfilling. If our persecutors are silenced, our leaders are godly, and the lost are being won to Christ, the body of Christ will expand and develop in wonderful ways. We will be allowed to live quiet lives in godliness and reverence.

Furthermore, *we* will change even as we pray for change in the lives of others. Often as we pray for others, God shows us ways in which we need to adjust our attitudes, move toward others with love, or soften our behavior. We must remain open to God's dealing with us, even as we pray for our enemies.

**3.** "Love suffers long and is kind; love does not envy; love does not parade itself, is not puffed up; does not behave rudely, does not seek its own, is not provoked, thinks no evil; does not rejoice in iniquity, but rejoices in the truth" (1 Corinthians 13:4–6). What are some examples you have seen of envy, parading oneself, being puffed up, seeking one's aims at the expense of others, and being easily provoked?

......................................................................................................
......................................................................................................
......................................................................................................
......................................................................................................
......................................................................................................
......................................................................................................

**4.** What are some specific examples of how love is the opposite of each of these?

......................................................................................................
......................................................................................................
......................................................................................................
......................................................................................................
......................................................................................................
......................................................................................................

# INITIAL STEPS FOR EFFECTIVE INTERCESSION

Each of us has had an experience in which we have prayed for other people and have not seen any results. When this happens, it is easy for us to become discouraged. However, rather than give up on our intercession in such cases, we would be wise to review our lives to see if we need to alter something in our actions and behaviors so that our prayers will be more effective. The following are six key principles for effective intercession.

*First, our prayers must flow from a heart filled with love, compassion, and forgiveness.* Our prayers are not effective if we have hearts filled with bitterness, resentment, or anger. In praying for others, we must first pray that we have God's love and compassion for others, and that we might forgive them fully.

*Second, we must view our prayers as the link between someone's need and God's resources.* As we pray for another person's need, God acts on that person's behalf. The responsibility to pray is an awesome one. He expects us to see needs and to pray about them. When we do not pray, others remain in need. The problem may not be their lack of faith or lack of relationship with the Father as much as it is our lack of prayer. So as you pray, ask the Lord to reveal to you the true needs of a person, not just the superficial or symptomatic needs. Ask Him to reveal the greatness of His love and power and to bring the person to wholeness.

*Third, we must identify with the need of the other person.* Compassion is feeling the full depth of another's need and being willing to help carry the spiritual burden of the other person. This is why we must pray for the Lord to reveal the deepest level of need in the person's life. When we see people with the eyes of Jesus and recognize that we have those same needs, our compassion is released. We pray with a new degree of understanding and depth of emotion.

**5.** "These things I command you, that you love one another" (John 15:17). Why did Jesus specifically command His followers to love one another? What are some practical ways that you can love others each and every day?

6. "Is anyone among you suffering? Let him pray. Is anyone cheerful? Let him sing psalms. Is anyone among you sick? Let him call for the elders of the church, and let them pray over him, anointing him with oil in the name of the Lord. And the prayer of faith will save the sick, and the Lord will raise him up" (James 5:13–15). What does this passage say about the connection between prayer and meeting the needs of others?

......................................................................................................

......................................................................................................

......................................................................................................

......................................................................................................

......................................................................................................

......................................................................................................

......................................................................................................

......................................................................................................

......................................................................................................

......................................................................................................

# FURTHER STEPS FOR EFFECTIVE INTERCESSION

*A fourth key for effective intercession is to always desire the highest good in another person's life.* The person's highest good may not be what the person is requesting or what we first think to pray. When we say to God, "I want what's best for this person," we must never add an "if," "and," or "but" to our prayer. We must take our hands off the person and let God put His hands on him. This is difficult to do, especially for parents who are praying for their children.

God may not reveal what His highest good is going to be for another person, but we can make it our prayer nonetheless. We do not need to know the full potential for blessing in another person's life to trust God to bring it to pass. Ultimately, God's highest good is *wholeness.* Jesus said repeatedly to those who were brought to Him, "Be made whole." Wholeness includes vibrancy and life in every domain—spirit, mind, body, emotions, relationships, and finances.

*Fifth, we must be willing to be part of the answer in meeting the other person's need.* When we are not willing to be used by God to meet another person's need, the Lord will not hear our prayers. We are actually voicing our prayer with a desire for isolation and separation—which is self-centeredness—and not with a desire to be a part of the greater body of Christ. Jesus touched lepers, the unclean, the desperately sick, and the dead. He never backed away from people who came to Him in need or passed them on to someone else for healing and deliverance. We are to follow His example.

*Sixth, we must be willing to persevere in prayer.* We must keep on praying for others, regardless of whether we see immediate results. The longer we pray for a person with compassion, the more tightly our hearts will be knit to that person. Prayer binds us together with a spiritual glue that is stronger than anything that mankind can ever create. It is a bond that will last into eternity.

**7.** "Bear one another's burdens, and so fulfill the law of Christ.... Let each one examine his own work, and then he will have rejoicing in himself alone, and not in another" (Galatians 6:2, 4). What part do you have to play in meeting the needs of others? What does it mean to "examine" your own work in this regard?

**8.** "So I say to you, ask, and it will be given to you; seek, and you will find; knock, and it will be opened to you. For everyone who asks receives, and he who seeks finds, and to him who knocks it will be opened" (Luke 11:9-10). What does this passage say about persisting in prayer? What is the promise given for those who choose to do this?

.................................................................................................................

.................................................................................................................

.................................................................................................................

.................................................................................................................

.................................................................................................................

.................................................................................................................

.................................................................................................................

.................................................................................................................

.................................................................................................................

.................................................................................................................

.................................................................................................................

# A CHALLENGE TO PRAY FOR OTHERS

I challenge you today to ask God to reveal three people for whom you should pray. Ask Him to show you three people who are suffering. Ask Him to give you His love and compassion for those people and to show you ways in which you might help carry their spiritual and emotional burdens, as well as ways in which you might be of assistance to them in practical ways. Then begin to pray for them. Ask God to make them whole, beginning with their deepest needs. It is not enough to know *how* to pray for others. You are required to also actually *pray* for them.

**9.** "I thank my God upon every remembrance of you, always in every prayer of mine making request for you all with joy, for your fellowship in the gospel from the first day until now" (Philippians 1:3–5). What words does Paul use to describe his prayers for others? What do these words teach regarding intercessory prayer?

10. Why does Paul make his requests "with joy"? What does this teach about praying for the needs of others?

## TODAY AND TOMORROW

*Today:* The Lord calls me to pray diligently
for the needs of others.

*Tomorrow:* This week, I will ask the Lord to show
me whom to pray for—and then I will do so regularly.

# CLOSING PRAYER

. . . . . . . . . . . . . . . . . . . . . . . . . . . . . . . . . . . . . . . . . . . . . . . .

*Father, thank You for all of the people You have raised up who have prayed for us—often without our even knowing. Today, we ask that you place three people on our hearts whom we will pray for this week. Let three names come to our minds . . . three people whose hurts, heartaches, and needs we are willing to share. We resolve to keep praying for these people until we see the answer come. We pledge that we are willing to take these principles we have learned and apply them to these people. Thank You, in advance, for the work You will do in their lives.*

# NOTES AND PRAYER REQUESTS

Use this space to write any key points, questions, or prayer requests from this week's study.

# TIME TO PRAY OR TIME TO ACT?

## IN THIS LESSON

*Learning:* After I pray . . . what do I do next?

*Growing:* What is the Lord calling me to do today?

Jesus was a man of intense and frequent prayer. The Gospels have numerous accounts of Him withdrawing to pray. Prayer is a thread that ran throughout His life and ministry. The disciples were men of prayer, as were members of the early church. When Peter was imprisoned by Herod, "constant prayer was offered to God for him by the church" (Acts 12:5).

The apostle Paul repeatedly stated that we must *always* be in prayer: "For God is my witness . . . that without ceasing I make mention of you always in my prayers" (Romans 1:9). "I thank my God upon every remembrance of you, always in every prayer of mine making request for you all with joy" (Philippians 1:3–4). "Pray without ceasing" (1 Thessalonians 5:17).

Prayer is the foundation for all good works, miracles, and spiritual fruitfulness. God desires to have a praying people! However, the Bible states there are times when we are not to *pray* but to *act*. Prayer must never be a substitute for speaking and acting toward others as the Holy Spirit desires. We must never hide behind a shield of prayer, saying to God, "I would obey You . . . but I'm too busy praying." Our lives are to be in balance: pray and do. Trust and obey. Hear and follow. We are to be active doers of God's Word (see James 1:22 and John 13:17).

One of the best examples of this is found in a story told in Joshua 7:1–13. The Lord had just given the Israelites a great victory at Jericho, so Joshua sent men to spy out the next target for conquest: the city of Ai. It wasn't nearly the city that Jericho was, yet the Israelites were soundly defeated. It was a serious setback that caused grief and fear to fill the Israelite camp.

**1.** "Now Joshua sent men from Jericho to Ai . . . and spoke to them, saying, 'Go up and spy out the country.' So the men went up and spied out Ai. And they returned to Joshua and said to him, 'Do not let all the people go up, but let about two or three thousand men go up and attack Ai. Do not weary all the people there, for the people of Ai are few'" (Joshua 7:2–3). What was the Israelites' attitude as they prepared to attack Ai?

**2.** There is no record of Joshua inquiring of the Lord before he launched this attack. What might have led to this oversight?

........................................................................................

........................................................................................

........................................................................................

........................................................................................

........................................................................................

# THE CAUSE OF THE DEFEAT

What was the difference in the approach the Israelites took at Jericho and Ai? *First, God gave Joshua a mandate to defeat Jericho and promised He would deliver the city to Joshua.* Furthermore, God gave Joshua the military strategy by which the victory was to be won (see Joshua 6). The victory belonged to the Lord, and He received full glory for it.

God is precise when He gives instructions. He doesn't deal with generalities. He uses specific methods for specific circumstances. Jericho is the only city in the Bible that was taken by the Israelites because the priests and the people carried the Ark of the Covenant around it once a day for six days and then seven times on the seventh day. God no doubt had a battle plan for Ai, but Joshua didn't wait to receive it. Joshua sent out spies just as he had for Jericho, and when they came back with a report that Ai could easily be taken, Joshua dispatched a few thousand men without consulting God. He relied solely on prideful human opinion.

*Second, God had commanded the people of Israel to not touch the "accursed things" of Jericho.* They were to take only vessels made of silver, gold, bronze, or iron for the treasury of the house of the Lord and burn the rest. Joshua gave clear instructions to the men of Israel (see Joshua 6:18). But a man named Achan did not obey. He brought accursed things into the camp, including a beautiful Babylonian garment. He also took 200 shekels of silver and wedges of gold for himself. He buried them in the ground inside his tent.

Had Joshua sought God's face before moving against Ai, the Lord would probably have revealed what Achan had done. The problem could have been resolved before any assault was made on Ai. If it had been, the Israelites would undoubtedly have been successful a second time—again, without any loss of Israelite life.

**3.** When have you moved ahead of God's plan and acted on your own without guidance from the Lord? What was the result?

**4.** "Be doers of the word, and not hearers only, deceiving yourselves" (James 1:22). What does it mean to be a "doer" of the Word? What does this involve?

## ASKING THE RIGHT QUESTION

When the men of Israel returned in defeat, Joshua turned immediately to prayer. He tore his garment (an act of grief) and he fell on his face in humiliation before the Ark of the Covenant. All the elders joined him in this act. Joshua basically cried out to God, "Why did You do this?"

Joshua asked the wrong question . . . though it is a question many of us also ask when trouble strikes us. Our first impulse is to blame God for the tragedy that is overwhelming us. The appropriate questions to ask are, "What did I do that was wrong? How did I get into this mess? What can I do to correct this situation?" Sometimes, we need to change a habit or correct a bad attitude. We may need to confront our own sin and error.

When Joshua had ceased pouring out his frustration to God, the Lord said, "Get up! Why do you lie thus on your face? Israel has sinned, and they have also transgressed My covenant which I commanded them" (Joshua 7:10-11). When we go to God in prayer, we must be willing to hear what God says. Often, people go to God in prayer, voice their petition, and never stop to hear back from God. In fact, they never even give it a thought that God might want to say something to them. We must wait when we voice our petitions to hear God's response. This is especially true when we are praying in the aftermath of a defeat. It is also vitally important that we do this anytime we find ourselves blaming God for our troubles. We must be willing to listen for His explanation—which often is a correction.

Once the Lord reveals what we need to correct, the time for prayer has ended. There is nothing more to be said—no excuses or attempts to justify what we have done. We must accept what the Lord says and move to obey Him. Our obedience may include asking Him to forgive us and to help us to obey Him. But our actions of obedience must follow quickly. There are usually amends to be made or specific actions to be taken that will help right the wrong.

In Joshua's case, he rose early the next morning, organized Israel by tribes, and discovered who had taken the accursed things. He moved quickly to correct the problem. In fact, he resolved the situation before the day ended. After the sin had been cleansed from the camp, the Lord said to Joshua, "Do not be afraid, nor be dismayed; take all the people of war with you, and arise, go up to Ai. See, I have given into your hand the king of Ai" (Joshua 8:1). When Joshua did as God commanded, the people were successful. No Israelite lives were lost, the city was brought to desolation, and there was great bounty added to the Israelite camp.

There are times when we will find it much easier to pray about our sins than to turn our back on them. It is easier to pray for another person than do something practical to help that person. It is easier to pray for our relationship with another person than to take steps toward reconciliation. It is easier to pray about our indebtedness than to curb our spending habits. But at these times, God calls us to get up off our knees and deal with the problems that we have created for ourselves. Only then will He bless us.

**5.** What question did Joshua ask the Lord after the Israelites suffered this defeat? What did God reveal to him was the *correct* question to ask?

**6.** What did God reveal about the Israelites' defeat? What did the people need to do before God gave them victory? How does this principle apply to your prayer life?

# FOUR PRINCIPLES FOR DECIDING WHETHER TO PRAY OR ACT

The story from Joshua gives us four key principles we can use to test whether we should keep praying or start acting. *First, there is a time to wait before God in prayer and a time to act.* The time to wait is when we do not have a clear direction from God to act. Until we know what to do regarding a specific circumstance, we should remain in prayer. The time to act is when the Lord reveals to us anything that needs to be changed in our lives. Sometimes the change is a new behavior that we need to develop or a new step that we are to take.

*Second, blaming God in prayer is a waste of time.* Anytime we hold God responsible for our troubles, we are in error. God does not do bad things *to* people. God does good things *for* people. He may have allowed our error to result in something bad in our lives, but He has allowed it so we might learn from it, correct the situation, and move forward to greater blessing. He may have allowed a tragic circumstance to occur, but He has a plan for good to come from it as we yield our lives to Him.

*Third, when God shows we are in error, we must correct it immediately.* We may need to ask the Lord how and when we should take specific actions, especially if someone else is involved, but we must take specific steps to correct the error immediately. Certainly we can pray as we take those steps—we don't have to be on our knees or in a secluded place to pray. Our prayers don't cease, but our period of waiting on the Lord should end at the moment that God reveals what we are to do. No excuses, and no delays.

*Fourth, we can't substitute prayer for action.* We should not compound our errors by thinking we can "pray the problem away." If God has revealed an error, it will not be resolved solely by prayer. His command to us is, "Deal with this!" We may not be able to achieve full reconciliation, arrive at a total solution, or meet the entirety of need through one action. We may need to deal with the problem, and then deal further with the problem, and then deal even further with the problem. Most problems are not created in a day or resolved in a day. Our prayer as we deal with the situation is to be constant: "Lord, give me courage to do this, give me wisdom to know how to do this, give me strength to persist in doing this." This kind of prayer complements our action. It is not a substitute for action.

God requires us to take initiative. We must have a zeal for doing what is right if His work in us is going to continue and if His kingdom is going to continue to be expanded. He asks us to pray so that He can guide our initiative, but He expects us to work, speak, exert, give, share—to *do*. If we fail to deal with a problem after God reveals it to us, we are cheating ourselves of future success. The roadblock to our success doesn't disappear. It remains until we attend to it. How much better to act on it quickly than to delay or to deny that the roadblock exists!

**7.** "Show me Your ways, O LORD; teach me Your paths. Lead me in Your truth and teach me, for You are the God of my salvation; on You I wait all the day" (Psalm 25:4–5). How does the Lord show us His ways and teach us His paths? Be specific.

**8.** Notice the metaphors in these verses: "paths," "ways," "lead me." What do each of these words and phrases suggest concerning praying and doing?

.................................................................................................

.................................................................................................

.................................................................................................

.................................................................................................

.................................................................................................

.................................................................................................

.................................................................................................

.................................................................................................

.................................................................................................

# A LIFE OF PRAYER

When we act on the problems the Lord reveals to us, we take one step closer to realizing the full potential that God has placed within us. We come closer to receiving more of the abundant blessings He has for us. We grow deeper in our relationship with Him, for we experience anew His mercy and loving forgiveness. We also have greater insight into the righteousness, justice, and perfection of God. We see with renewed insight the glory that belongs to God alone.

God repeatedly calls His people to come to Him. We first come to Him when we recognize our sinfulness, casting ourselves on His mercy to forgive us and impart His Holy Spirit. Daily we are to come to Him for guidance in making choices and decisions, for forgiveness for our sins, for correction and teaching, for deliverance from evil, and to voice our petitions for protection and provision. On a daily basis, the Holy Spirit imparts the ability to live godly lives.

Our relationship with our heavenly Father grows and deepens as we enter into a life of daily prayer. We can devise no other means to this growth through our own strength and ability. God has made no other provision for it. Prayer is the means to intimacy with God.

The most important lessons about prayer that you can ever learn are learned by praying.

So I encourage you today to renew your commitment to talk with God on a daily basis. Listen closely to Him. Hear His thoughts and plans for you. These are thoughts and plans for your good. Delight in your relationship with the Lord. For He delights in you.

**9.** "Do not be wise in your own eyes; fear the LORD and depart from evil. It will be health to your flesh, and strength to your bones" (Proverbs 3:7–8). What does it mean to be "wise in your own eyes"? How is this avoided?

**10.** Why is it necessary to avoid being wise in your own eyes in order to understand the Lord's direction in life?

## TODAY AND TOMORROW

*Today:* The Lord wants me to pray and to do—to be living in obedience to His Word.

*Tomorrow:* I will ask the Lord specifically what action He wants me to take this week.

# CLOSING PRAYER

*Heavenly Father, sometimes when we seek You in prayer . . . we overlook the fact You have already instructed us on what to do. At these times, help us to receive Your blessings by getting up from our knees and dealing with the situation head-on. We recognize today that praying involves initiative. Let us take that initiative when You've called us to move and recognize Your guidance as a gentle encouragement to lift us up, to build us up, and to help shape us into the likeness of Christ. We want to always be moving forward in our relationship with You.*

# Notes and Prayer Requests

Use this space to write any key points, questions, or prayer requests from this week's study.

# PRAYER IS WHERE THE BATTLE IS WON

## IN THIS LESSON

*Learning:* Why is prayer necessary for winning the battles of life?

*Growing:* Where can I find people to assist me in my prayer life?

We have reached the final session of this study on one of the most important topics we could ever cover: *prayer.* As we've seen, prayer in one sense is extraordinarily simple—it is communicating with God. It is talking with God and listening as He talks back. On the other hand, we have also seen there is a remarkable depth and breadth when it comes to the practice of prayer as a discipline in our lives.

We have studied the importance of praying with authority. We have seen how fasting provides a boost to our prayers. We have learned about what it means to pray in God's will and what we can do when it seems like our prayers go unanswered. In this final session, I want to remind you again of the critical importance of prayer in your life. Why? Because you are in a battle. I am as well. Each of us who serve as members of God's kingdom are in a battle against the forces of evil in this world. I hope you will hear me on this critical point: *prayer is our key to victory in that battle.* Prayer is the key to victory in our spiritual lives.

## ENDURING THE BATTLES OF LIFE

I want to begin this final lesson by examining a story found in Exodus. This passage contains a principle for us to consider when it comes to understanding the heart of prayer:

> Now Amalek came and fought with Israel in Rephidim. And Moses said to Joshua, "Choose us some men and go out, fight with Amalek. Tomorrow I will stand on the top of the hill with the rod of God in my hand." So Joshua did as Moses said to him, and fought with Amalek. And Moses, Aaron, and Hur went up to the top of the hill. And so it was, when Moses held up his hand, that Israel prevailed; and when he let down his hand, Amalek prevailed. But Moses' hands became heavy; so they took a stone and put it under him, and he sat on it. And Aaron and Hur supported his hands, one on one side, and the other on the other side; and his hands were steady until the going down of the sun. So Joshua defeated Amalek and his people with the edge of the sword (Exodus 17:8–13).

The Israelites had recently experienced the exodus from Egypt. They were numerous in terms of people and wealthy in terms of resources, having plundered Egypt on the way out. They were also strung out across a large area geographically. For those reasons, the Amalekites began conducting raids against the outskirts and stragglers of the Israelite convoy.

In response, Moses put Joshua in charge of the army and said, "Choose us some men and go out, fight with Amalek" (verse 9). However, Moses joined the battle in a different way. He went up to the top of a nearby mountain to pray—to hold up his hands before heaven.

Like the Israelites, you have walked through many battles in your life, and at times you have certainly come out bloody, torn, and even defeated. You have faced financial problems, you have gone through battles in your home, you have gone through battles in your vocation, and you have gone through battles in your relationships with other people. So, in this lesson we will examine three principles that will assist you in those battles and help you find victory.

**1.** What is a battle that you are currently facing when you need to experience victory?

.................................................................................................................
.................................................................................................................
.................................................................................................................
.................................................................................................................
.................................................................................................................
.................................................................................................................
.................................................................................................................
.................................................................................................................

**2.** What prayers have you been offering to God as you go through this time?

.................................................................................................................
.................................................................................................................
.................................................................................................................
.................................................................................................................
.................................................................................................................
.................................................................................................................
.................................................................................................................
.................................................................................................................

# LIFE'S BATTLES ARE WON THROUGH PRAYER

*The first principle is that the battles of our lives are won or lost in the place of prayer.* For most people this is a difficult statement to believe, because most people look at the outward actions and activities when they evaluate what is going right and wrong. For example, most people look at the leadership of a company—their organization and strategies and plans. Or they look at a person and evaluate success based on intelligence or attractiveness or personality.

But that's not where the real battle takes place. The real battles of life, the important battles, are won or lost to the degree that people are willing to get on their knees before God and seek His face. Why is this? Because the enemy we often believe we are fighting against is not the *real* enemy. When we come up against conflicts and battles, we tend to think we are fighting against finances or temptations or addictions or difficult relationships. But those are merely the *symptoms* of the battle. They do not represent the real enemy.

The real enemy behind everything is Satan. The real enemy is the demonic forces of evil that attack and seek to ensnare and thwart the purposes of God. The Lord wants us to recognize that we are in a *spiritual* battle—and the only way to win a spiritual battle is by equipping spiritual weapons. Specifically, this involves prayer.

This is what Moses and Joshua learned on that day of the battle. Yes, the Israelite army was directly engaged in the struggle against the Amalekites. But it wasn't the swords and shields of the Israelites that determined their victory or defeat. It was Moses' intercession through prayer. As long as Moses held up his hands toward heaven—including holding the rod God had given Him as a sign of His supernatural power—the Israelites pushed forward to victory. But when Moses lowered his hands, the Israelites were pushed back toward defeat.

The principle here is that God wants us to fight our battles in the prayer room, not out in the public forums of our lives.

**3.** Where and when do you typically come before God in prayer?

................................................................

................................................................

................................................................

................................................................

................................................................

................................................................

**4.** When you face conflicts and troubles in life, do you tend to focus more on the private battle through prayer or the public aspects of those conflicts? Why?

................................................................

................................................................

................................................................

................................................................

................................................................

................................................................

# WE WILL GROW FAINTHEARTED

*The second principle is that when we face life's battles, we will grow fainthearted at times.* No matter how strong we think we may be—including spiritual strength—we will falter.

Just look at Moses. He was the greatest statesman that has ever lived on this earth. There he was, holding up the rod as a symbol of God's intercession before those two armies. But after a while, his hands got heavy. They got so heavy that eventually he dropped them. When they were down by his side, he suddenly noticed a change in the battle. Amalek and his forces began to defeat the people of God, so up went Moses' hands again. But then he tired again. Up they went . . . and down they went. Even Moses' strength grew faint.

In the Gospel of Luke, we read that Jesus told a parable about a persistent widow "that men always ought to pray and not lose heart"

(18:1). The problem is that we all do lose heart at times. Not all of the time . . . but it will happen at some point. We even lose heart when it comes to prayer—which was the point of Jesus telling the parable. There will be times when we have prayed for something so long and so hard that we just don't feel like praying any more. You know you should pray, but you have lost the will. Maybe you even think, "Lord, You aren't doing anything, so why should I keep praying when nothing seems to happen?"

Satan jumps up and down with glee when we reach that point—when we grow fainthearted in our prayers. He knows the immense importance of prayer in the battles of life. He wants nothing more than to convince us prayer unnecessary and simply does not work.

I have learned over the years there are some battles that you just have to pray through in the same way you would tunnel through a mountain. You just have to keep hanging in there, telling God about it, trusting Him, believing Him, thanking Him, and praising Him—even though everything you see and hear says "defeat, defeat, defeat." Why? Because if you listen closely, you can hear God saying, "Victory is on the way. You're almost through."

We all grow fainthearted, but we must not let the loss of our strength result in the loss of our prayers. Keep praying.

**5.** What are some of the symptoms a person might experience if he or she grows fainthearted during a spiritual battle?

**6.** When have you lost faith in the power or the necessity of prayer?

.............................................................................

.............................................................................

.............................................................................

.............................................................................

.............................................................................

# WE ALL NEED PARTNERS IN PRAYER

*The third principle is that we all need prayer partners to secure the victory.* I have made the case that we are all going to suffer faintheartedness at different points in our lives. During these times, we need the help and support of others to keep us moving forward in the battle.

Prayer partners are people like Aaron and Hur in the story told in Exodus. When God sent Moses up on the top of a mountain, He knew that Moses couldn't hold up his hands for very long. This is why He also instructed Moses take two others with him.

Remember how God built His church: "By this all will know that you are My disciples, if you have love for one another" (John 13:35). People who love each other can depend on each other. People who love each other are loyal to each other. People who love each other encourage one another. People who love each other want to build up one another. People who love each other are available to one another. God has built the church on this interdependence. Even as we depend on God, we also depend on one another.

When the battle gets tough, you don't need people around you who say, "I told you so." You don't need people to come close and then advise you to pull yourself up by your own bootstraps. You don't need people who argue with you and try to convince you that everything would be much better if you would just approach the battle the way they believe is right.

Instead, you need an Aaron and a Hur—especially in your prayer life. You need people who can hold you up when you begin to droop.

You need people who can stand with you and support you when you feel discouraged or when you lose heart.

The Bible states, "Though one may be overpowered by another, two can withstand him. And a threefold cord is not quickly broken" (Ecclesiastes 4:12). We can talk to God as individuals, and there is value in that. Two can talk to God together, and that is productive as well. But there's something special about three men or three women on their face before God lifting one another up—especially as we engage in these critical battles in our lives.

**7.** Do you find it easy or difficult to invite others into your prayer life? Why?

**8.** When you are in the middle of a battle, where do you typically turn for help?

## SELECTING YOUR PRAYER PARTNERS

An important truth to consider is that not just anyone can serve as an Aaron or a Hur in your life. Don't turn to just any friend or family member for this kind of support—this kind of mutual strengthening. You need to find people you can trust. You need to find people who will be *effective* in holding you up, rather than people who will ultimately drag you down.

With that in mind, let me offer four characteristics that you should look for when you are seeking out an Aaron or a Hur in your life. *First, find people who are spiritually minded.* Look for people who are interested in seeking God, are willing to obey God, and have chosen to trust Him. You need people in your life who want God's best for you, not their best. You need people speaking to you who will objectively say, "I want God's best for your life."

*Second, seek out people who are willing to accept you as you are, no matter what problem you may be facing.* You need people who can evaluate your circumstances and not think any less of you or any more of you. You need people who will accept you as you are and know that God has put them on your side to lift you up.

I have these types of prayer partners in my life, and it is wonderful. When I fail, I know my Aaron and my Hur won't abandon me. They won't think less of me. Rather, they will come beside me and pray, "Lord God Almighty, we are in prayer for our brother that You will give him wisdom to know what to do. Give him strength for his body. Give him energy for his spirit. Give him faith to trust You." Find people like these who will accept you as you are and not make you feel like you need to pretend you have it all together.

*Third, find people in your life who care.* You need people who have compassionate hearts and can feel what you feel. Another way to say this is that you need people in your life who genuinely and truly love you—people who will give themselves to you without asking anything in return. Genuine love always asks what's best for the other. "What can I do for this person I love? How can I pour out my life into his life in a way that lifts him up?"

*Finally, find people who are faithful.* You don't need those who will only pray with you when it is convenient. No, find those individuals who will come when you need them to come. Find those people who will pray when you need them to pray—who recognize that your need is so great that they are willing to stop whatever they are doing to come by your side and cry out to God with you and on your behalf. Those are the people you need.

Prayer is the greatest key to victory in the battles of your life. Apart from prayer, you are fighting in your own strength against Satan and his forces. This is not a battle you can win on your own—you need spiritual power! You also need the strength and support of others who know you and love you and stand ready to lift you up. When you understand those truths, you will go a long way toward deepening your prayer life in the ways that matter most.

**9.** Who might be an Aaron or a Hur in your life?

**10.** Who are some people you can serve and support through mutual prayer?

## TODAY AND TOMORROW

*Today:* I am ready to make prayer the key weapon when
I fight against conflicts and struggles in my life.

*Tomorrow:* I am ready to serve as an Aaron or a Hur
to those who are the most important to me and need my
help through prayer.

# CLOSING PRAYER

*Lord, thank You for the victory, liberty, and freedom that is ours in Christ. We know we do not have to surrender to the enemy. We do not have to give up. We do not have to go down in defeat. We can live moment by moment, day by day, trusting in the power of the Holy Spirit who indwells us. He is our victory. He is our peace. He is our strength. Sink these truths deep into our hearts and give us initiative to act them out through faith. We pray this in Jesus' name.*

# Notes and Prayer Requests

Use this space to write any key points, questions, or prayer requests from this week's study.

# LEADER'S GUIDE

Thank you for choosing to lead your group through this Bible study from Dr. Charles F. Stanley on *Deepening Your Prayer Life*. The rewards of being a leader are different from those of participating, and it is our prayer that your own walk with Jesus will be deepened by this experience. During the twelve lessons in this study, you will be helping your group members explore key themes about how to interact on a daily basis with God through Dr. Stanley's teachings and review questions that will encourage group discussion. There are multiple components in this section that can help you structure your lessons and discussion time, so please be sure to read and consider each one.

## BEFORE YOU BEGIN

Before your first meeting, make sure your group members each have a copy of *Deepening Your Prayer Life* so they can follow along in the study guide and have their answers written out ahead of time. Alternately, you can hand out the study guides at your first meeting and give the group members some time to look over the material and ask any preliminary questions. During your first meeting, be sure to send a sheet around the room and have the members write down their name, phone number, and email address so you can keep in touch with them during the week.

To ensure everyone has a chance to participate in the discussion, the ideal size for a group is around eight to ten people. If there are more than ten people, break up the bigger group into smaller subgroups. Make sure the members are committed to participating each week, as this will help create stability and help you better prepare the structure of the meeting.

At the beginning of each meeting, you may wish to start the group time by asking the group members to provide their initial reactions to the material they have read during the week. The goal is to just get the group members' preliminary thoughts—so encourage them at this point to keep their answers brief. Ideally, you want everyone in the group to get a chance to share some of their thoughts, so try to keep the responses to a minute or less.

Give the group members a chance to answer, but tell them to feel free to pass if they wish. With the rest of the study, it's generally not a good idea to have everyone answer every question—a free-flowing discussion is more desirable. But with the opening icebreaker questions, you can go around the circle. Encourage shy people to share, but don't force them. Also, try to keep any one person from dominating the discussion so everyone will have the opportunity to participate.

# WEEKLY PREPARATION

As the group leader, there are a few things you can do to prepare for each meeting:

- *Be thoroughly familiar with the material in the lesson.* Make sure you understand the content of each lesson so you know how to structure the group time and are prepared to lead the group discussion.

- *Decide, ahead of time, which questions you want to discuss.* Depending on how much time you have each week, you may not be able to reflect on every question. Select specific questions that you feel will evoke the best discussion.

- *Take prayer requests.* At the end of your discussion, take prayer requests from your group members and then pray for one another.

- *Pray for your group.* Pray for your group members throughout the week and ask God to lead them as they study His Word.

- *Bring extra supplies to your meeting.* The members should bring their own pens for writing notes, but it's a good idea to have extras available for those who forget. You may also want to bring paper and additional Bibles.

# STRUCTURING THE GROUP DISCUSSION TIME

You will need to determine with your group how long you want to meet each week so you can plan your time accordingly. Generally, most groups like to meet for either sixty minutes or ninety minutes, so you could use one of the following schedules:

| SECTION | 60 Minutes | 90 Minutes |
|---|---|---|
| WELCOME (group members arrive and get settled) | 5 minutes | 10 minutes |
| ICEBREAKER (group members share their initial thoughts regarding the content in the lesson) | 10 minutes | 15 minutes |
| DISCUSSION (discuss the Bible study questions you selected ahead of time) | 35 minutes | 50 minutes |
| PRAYER/CLOSING (pray together as a group and dismiss) | 10 minutes | 15 minutes |

As the group leader, it is up to you to keep track of the time and keep things moving according to your schedule. If your group is having a good discussion, don't feel the need to stop and move on to the next question. Remember, the purpose is to pull together ideas and share unique insights on the lesson. Encourage everyone to participate, but don't be concerned if certain group members are more quiet. They may just be internally reflecting on the questions and need time to process their ideas before they can share them.

# GROUP DYNAMICS

Leading a group study can be a rewarding experience for you and your group members—but that doesn't mean there won't be challenges. Certain members may feel uncomfortable in discussing topics that they consider very personal and might be afraid of being called on. Some members might have disagreements on specific issues. To help prevent these scenarios, consider establishing the following ground rules:

- If someone has a question that may seem off topic, suggest that it is discussed at another time, or ask the group if they are okay with addressing that topic.

- If someone asks a question to which you do not know the answer, confess that you don't know and move on. If you feel comfortable, you can invite the other group members to give their opinions or share their comments based on personal experience.

- If you feel like a couple of people are talking much more than others, direct questions to people who may not have shared yet. You could even ask the more dominating members to help draw out the quiet ones.

- When there is a disagreement, encourage the members to process the matter in love. Invite members from opposing sides to evaluate their opinions and consider the ideas of the other members. Lead the group through Scripture that addresses the topic, and look for common ground.

When issues arise, encourage your group to follow these words from Scripture: "Love one another" (John 13:34), "If it is possible, as much as it depends on you, live peaceably with all men" (Romans 12:18), "Whatever things are true…noble…pure…lovely…if there is any virtue and if there is anything praiseworthy—meditate on these things" (Philippians 4:8), and "Be swift to hear, slow to speak, slow to wrath" (James 1:19). This will make your group time more rewarding and beneficial for everyone who attends.

Thank you again for your willingness to lead your group. May God reward your efforts and dedication, equip you to guide your group in the weeks ahead, and make your time together in *Deepening Your Prayer Life* fruitful for His kingdom.

# Also Available in the
# Charles F. Stanley Bible Study Series

The Charles F. Stanley Bible Study Series is a unique approach
to Bible study, incorporating biblical truth, personal insights,
emotional responses, and a call to action. Each study draws on
Dr. Stanley's many years of teaching the guiding principles found
in God's Word, showing how we can apply them in practical
ways to every situation we face. This edition of the series has
been completely revised and updated, and includes two
brand-new lessons from Dr. Stanley.

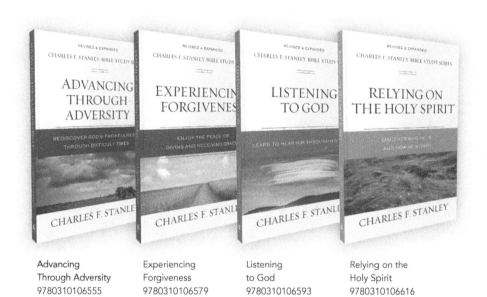

| Advancing Through Adversity | Experiencing Forgiveness | Listening to God | Relying on the Holy Spirit |
|---|---|---|---|
| 9780310106555 | 9780310106579 | 9780310106593 | 9780310106616 |

Available now at your favorite bookstore.
More volumes coming soon.

THOMAS NELSON
Since 1798

Printed in the USA
CPSIA information can be obtained
at www.ICGtesting.com
LVHW011354241223
767279LV00011B/125